THE
THEATRE
TEAM

Recent Titles in
Contributions in Drama and Theatre Studies

THE
THEATRE
TEAM

Playwright, Producer, Director, Designers, and Actors

EDITED BY
Jeane Luere and Sidney Berger

Contributions in Drama and Theatre Studies, Number 80

Greenwood Press
Westport, Connecticut • London

Library of Congress Cataloging-in-Publication Data

The theatre team : playwright, producer, director, designers, and
   actors / edited by Jeane Luere and Sidney Berger.
       p.   cm.—(Contributions in drama and theatre studies, ISSN
   0163–3821 ; no. 80)
     Includes bibliographical references and index.
     ISBN 0–313–30050–X (alk. paper)
     1. Theater—Production and direction.   2. Playwriting.
   3. Theaters—Stage-setting and scenery.   4. Acting.   I. Luere,
   Jeane.   II. Berger, Sidney.   III. Series.
   PN2053.T44   1998
   792'.023—dc21   97–15298

British Library Cataloguing in Publication Data is available.

Library of Congress Catalog Card Number: 97–15298
ISBN: 0–313–30050–X
ISSN: 0163–3821

First published in 1998

Greenwood Press, 88 Post Road West, Westport, CT 06881
An imprint of Greenwood Publishing Group, Inc.

Printed in the United States of America

∞™

The paper used in this book complies with the
Permanent Paper Standard issued by the National
Information Standards Organization (Z39.48–1984).

10 9 8 7 6 5 4 3 2 1

To Eric Sagel and Jeff Piquette for editorial
insight and technical proficiency

A play in a book is only the shadow of a play and not even a clear shadow of it. . . . The printed script of a play is hardly more than an architect's blueprint of a house not yet built or [a house] built and destroyed. The color, the grace and levitation, the structural pattern in motion, the quick interplay of living beings, suspended like fitful lightning in a cloud, these things are the play, not words on paper nor thoughts and ideas of an author.

—Tennessee Williams, Afterword to *Camino Real*

Despite the energy and presence of a stage production, the only perfect performance is that on the page with the play neither altered nor disproved. Plays—good ones, at any rate—are literature, and the pervasive notion that a play comes to full life only on stage speaks either of an inability to realize a production through reading or [of] a flawed play.

[Still,] given a choice, I would prefer an endlessly running, perfect production of a play of mine over [its] publication.

—Edward Albee, Introduction to
Selected Plays of Edward Albee

Contents

PART III: THE PLAYWRIGHT

PART IV: THE DESIGNER

PART V: THE ACTOR

Photo essay follows page 72.

Acknowledgments

For the theatre experience and discernment of my advisory editor, Sidney Berger, Director of the School of Theatre, University of Houston, I am both indebted and appreciative. For the enthusiasm and patience of the University of Houston's Sandy Judice, I am grateful. Here at the University of Northern Colorado, Pat Chandler, Office Manager of the English Department, has been indispensable during the book's final stages.

Administrative assistant Lynda Groves, assistant lab manager Peggy Hutton, and technical consultant Michelle Norton have made this volume an actuality. I also owe an academic debt to theatre professors through the decades and to long-established texts on script and performance that I encountered as student, guest professor, observer, and critic.

Introduction: The Theatre Team: Taking the Play to the Stage

Theatre is an art whose essence defies definition. Trying to summarize "theatre" is an old and testy exercise that probes the symbiotic relationship between playscript and performance. To move a playscript to the stage, its production team considers a staging from a broad spectrum of possibilities, ranging from a conventional to a radical approach. Though an unconventional staging of an author's script may please some audiences, a sanctified rather than radical and elastic approach to text may be the preference of traditional respecters of drama (Brustein 1994, 29).

Some viewers of innovative stagings "adapted to modern sensibilities" would prefer reading a play rather than watching its "temporal manifestations" from a theatre seat (Goldstein 1990, xiv). Hence the journey of a page to the stage is as touchy to audiences as to the playwright, producer, director, designers, and actors who make up our theatre teams.

Cautious references to the challenges in moving a play to the stage have appeared throughout theatre history. Vsevelod Meyerhold (1874–1940), an influential Russian director of the Moscow Art Theatre, regarded scripts as materials "in need of molding and reworking" as producers and their teams took them toward performance (Meyerhold 1982, 577).[1] Meyerhold envisioned the process of production as similar to the launching of a rocket: The rocket represents "text," and the path of the rocket from sphere to sphere suggests the text's progression toward the audience. The launching starts with a playwright; soon the playwright falls off, and the director takes the play and its actors onward; then the director falls off, and the actors must take the play away from the director and make it their own. Finally, in a sense, the actors fall off, and the play belongs to the audience. In each of these stages, stress and change accompany the molding and reworking of the script. Producer Richard Rodgers (1978) described the production process in *Musical Stages: An Autobiography*: "On the way to an audience, [playwrights and production teams] are constantly polishing and making changes; through trial and error they learn what makes dialogue funny or touching and what makes material not only suitable but remembered" (41). Like today's producers, Rodgers took plays on the road for extensive tryout-tours until he saw no need for more amendment. Rodgers' policy, however, was that after a play's opening, the performance should not be frozen: "It can't be put into a can like a movie or a television program to be taken out and shown without change" (266). Rather, he cautioned, producers must "keep the production fresh" by requiring frequent rehearsals to ensure that future audiences get "the best performance possible" (266).

Contemporary theatre teams seem bemused by conflicting theories on playtext and performance. Views of writers like Tennessee Williams and Edward Albee, reprinted in the epigraph, will clash if read cursorily. Williams (1953) wrote that drama is "*not* words on paper nor thoughts and ideas of an author" (xii). His words suggest that authors' pages themselves cannot qualify as drama because only in performance can words be embodied with sound and fury. His reflection could be misconstrued to disdain text. Yet Edward Albee (1987), in *Selected Plays*, wrote, "The only perfect performance is that on the page with the play neither altered nor disproved" (vii), negating the notion that only on stage do plays come to full life. Albee expects readers of well-written plays to "realize a production" themselves by forming visions as they read the scripted words (vii). Despite his dry assertions on the adequacy of a careful reading of a published text, Albee will admit that, "Given a choice, I would prefer an endlessly running, perfect production of a play of mine over [its] publication" (Albee 1987, vii). If members of a production team study these reflections closely, they will find that both writers want a play envisioned fully, whether through a reading of its pages or a viewing of its performance.

A playscript requires this full envisioning because its pages hold both explicit and implicit clues to how the work should be performed. The entire theatre team will need to imagine "what the dramatist's script might look like in performance, projecting in the mind's eye an image of the setting, the props, the movements, gestures, facial expressions, and vocal intonations of the characters" (Klaus, Gilbert, and Field 1991, 1). These efforts at interpreting the text for the stage begin as soon as a producer takes an option on a writer's script, then signs and secures financial backers for the project (Engel 1977, 151).

As the theatre team begins its work with the script, it will be constantly aware of a sequential link between the playwright's initial visions and the words that record them on the pages. If creativity supplies a playwright's mind with a picture *before* it provides the word with which to record it as text, then the playwright's words on a page are a map to that vision. Director, actor, and designer can capitalize on the map to find and reembody the playwright's initial picturing.

In his book, *The Making of a Musical*, Lehman Engel (1977) writes, "It is certainly true that when or if the author's show is actually put on stage, its 'look' will be considerably altered by the interpretive talents of the stage director and his collaboration with scenic and costume designers" (142). Bona fide productions, however, will always presuppose a collaborative search by theatre teams to identify the mental pictures that preceded the writer's words. This search of a playscript is a multifaceted and risky business and often a cause of anxiety for playwrights who must abandon a script to production; yet dedicated theatre teams can allay authors' uneasiness over their scripts' staging by exercising scrupulous judgment to ensure that viewers will grasp the author's dramatic intent. Whether a production group's status is professional, regional, or academic, this ethical assumption should characterize all staging policy.

The first stage of a near-perfect journey will be a careful reading of the script to get the playwright's scripted messages (Klaus, Gilbert, and Field 1991, 1). This effort seems akin to that of musicians studying sheets of music before a performance. Directors of orchestras are not wholly free to follow their inclinations as they conduct the pages of a symphony. Although they do have occasion for artistic expression, they must stay within the composer's designations for volume, rhythm, and tone printed on the sheets. Notations for diminuendo or crescendo, retardando or accelerando, for intervals of rest between notes, and for scripted dissonances, must all be heeded. Just so, the pages of drama do not give actors *carte blanche*. Playwrights imbed their intentions in their lines, relying on syntax and phrasing to indicate rhetorical pauses, on metrical patterns to control rhythm, and on euphony or cacophony to govern sound quality.

With this stress on staying within a script's intentions, performance teams might well question where their own artistry comes in, and under what sets of circumstances, if any, they might use their discretion to adjust an action or modify a stage moment. The playwright's in-text stage directions themselves may open up opportunities for interpretation. As in music, where a composer prints the phrase "cadenza ad lib" at a double bar to encourage performers to insert a cadenza of their own, playwrights leave space for interesting options. Stage directions may "suggest" rather than "indicate" an action or reaction, with words to the effect that "Perhaps this actress can . . ." rather than "Here, this actress should...." Or a playwright might suggest options for dressing the production's sets, props, and costumes. Opportunity for artistic expression also arises when teams must stretch financial resources and physical facilities creatively to meet the needs of the text.

Because these decisions on adjustments and substitutions will demand the team's taste and discretion, each section of this volume contains profiles of specific stagings wherein teams exercised judgment during production. Subjective-objective deadlocks ensued only if the team overpowered the script by grossly exploiting its authority to modify and adjust, or failed to collaborate smoothly during staging. These specific examples can be guidelines that avert malfunctioning.

The Theatre Team stresses the need for collaboration and communication among the members of the theatre team during their staging of the playscript. Before the journey of script to stage begins, the organization responsible for selecting the play and the style of its production must first reach a consensus on its *raison d'état*, its purpose in approaching an audience (to entertain, to elevate, to inform or reform). Because the goals and modes of production since mid-century are still evolving, theatre teams must remain conversant with shifts in forms and styles of drama, in techniques of staging, and in authority and responsibility of members of theatre teams. Though evolution in the roles of producer, playwright, and director has been neither uniform nor evenly paced, this volume demonstrates that change itself can provide theatre teams with the impetus for inspiration and creation.

In part, a theatre team's necessity to make independent and effective judgments in staging will depend upon how much consultation is possible with the playwright during production. One axiom—"No one knows the play so well as the playwright"—seems valid and useful *if* authors are at hand. The amount of discussion and guidance a team can expect will depend upon predetermined factors: (1) whether the playscript is a new one whose author, vitally involved in its interpretation, is present during production-rehearsals; (2) whether the play is beyond its tryouts and premiere, with its author, though still possessed of full legal authority over its interpretation, seldom available for collaboration with the team at rehearsals; or (3) whether the play is considered in the common domain, beyond the prescribed period for copyright protection of deceased playwrights' works.

With or without the presence of the playwright, success in moving the play to the stage will reward theatre teams who have collaborated well, who have visualized the pages, and who have agreed on the most convincing style in which to stage them. Smooth interaction between each producer, director, designer, and actor can win a place for the play amid what critics call "the poetry of the theatre" (Copeau 1913, reprinted in Brockett 1982, 578).

Through this text's examples of both troubled and smooth interaction among those who have produced drama since mid-century, *The Theatre Team* stresses clearly delegated authority and responsibility in production roles as teams interpret, rehearse, and present plays on our stages.

NOTE

1. Vsevelod Meyerhold's concepts on theatre, including his graphic comparison of production to the launching of a rocket, are discussed in Oscar Brockett, *History of the Theatre*, 4th ed. (Boston: Allyn and Bacon, 1982), 577.

PART I
THE PRODUCER

1

The Producer's Role

Some producers prefer to work quietly behind the scenes. Others, practically from the beginning, tend to be part of the show.
—Howard Kissel, *David Merrick: The Abominable Showman (The Unauthorized Biography)*

Throughout theatre history, traditional concepts of the role of producer have shifted rather than remained constant. Today, a precise demarcation of producers' functions seems crucial to the steady movement of a play toward an audience. To acknowledge that good producers, whether in commercial, regional, or academic venues, are eager to acquire valuable playscripts for development is easy; to define those producers' roles takes finesse (Engel 1977, 149). The responsibilities of theatre producers, especially in regional or academic venues, include planning the theatre's performance season as well as developing ongoing, related projects. One event might be the presentation of an annual Shakespeare Festival, or the planning of a special program to spotlight a significant community event. One academic theatre group, the University of Houston's School of Theatre, cosponsored a production with the Houston International Festival Committee to celebrate the quinquecentennial of the discovery of America. Producers may have as their responsibility the institution of a series of performances geared to families and children. For special projects like these, the producer must envision a concept, negotiate its approval, and market it for an audience.

For a regular performance season, a producer's functions range across a production hierarchy. In the past, producers had taken over roles usually ascribed to directors, assuming a measure of control over interpretation of the playscript itself, attending rehearsals regularly, and at times selecting and coaching actors. By mid-century, figures like David Merrick, Peter Hall, Robert Whitehead, and Hal Prince had become legends in theatre history, their names linked as inextricably with specific productions as were the names of the actors. In the last quarter of our century, producers have less often become indisputable kings of theatre with thrones in both management and artistic realms of performance (Engel 1977, 151). Today we have clearer separation between producer and director roles.

Typically producers search for new playscripts, study them closely, then acquire those they like by negotiating with a playwright or his agent. If the producer's efforts succeed, contacts (re: options) will be initiated with backers to fund the developing project (Engel 1977, 151). The producer and his staff then oversee the administrative and financial affairs of the theatre, develop its season, and organize publicity campaigns to draw audiences.

A more comprehensive statement of the role of producers, however, includes specific functions that vary within each major category of American theatre. Today's theatre venues can be loosely classified as commercial, regional, and academic. Earlier classifications bore the label "professional" in place of "commercial" to refer to what is still sometimes called "the National Theatre" on New York City's Broadway, Off-Broadway, and Off-Off Broadway. Yet the term *professional*, if it excludes regional theatre, now seems inappropriate; many community and semi-professional entities, with subsidies from government and large foundations, have achieved professional status. Examples are Houston's Alley Theatre, San Francisco's Magic Theatre, Minneapolis's Tyrone Guthrie Theatre, and Washington D.C.'s Arena Stage. Even within the three major classifications just noted, the functions of the producer have not been constant; typically they shift with time and individual circumstance.

In commercial theatre, a producer (individual or group) usually arranges financial support and provides physical management for production. The producer obtains rights to the play, finds backers, and develops the project; he or she hires a director who will take the play from script to stage, hires the cast, rents the theatre, and in a sense, "owns" the production. The producer also markets the play, handling programs, tickets, advertising, and other public relations to retrieve the backers' production costs and show a solid profit.

In the second category of theatre, that of regional or repertory venues, the notion of a "producer" has largely been replaced by two figures: artistic director and managing director. The group's artistic director interacts with the Board of Trustees and the Governors of the Theatre. The artistic director plans the season's program, obtains the options to produce the desired playscripts, selects directors for the season's offering, or perhaps directs one or more plays. He or she may also interpret the playscript, share in matters of casting, and maintain a staff of designers and technicians adequate for staging the season's plays. The association's managing director interacts with the artistic director and needs a strong background in fiscal areas related to the performing arts (Stephen Baker 1994, 1). He or she negotiates all contracts with actors and Equity, securing office space and theatre space when necessary. He or she also oversees publicity, marketing, and public relations (Stephen Baker 1994, 1).

In academic theatre, control of production rests with the Director of the School (or Department) of Theatre Arts, with the financial aspect of the producer role metaphorically replaced by the university's budgetary appropriation. In rare instances, the university may collaborate with an outside entity such as a festival committee or other community group to share financial backing for a particular event. The Director of the School of Theatre (or Chair of the Drama Department) must assume, with his or her staff, the other production functions—selecting the play, publicizing it, marketing it to advantage. Arrangements for photographs, radio or TV releases, ticket sales and reservations, mailings to subscribers, and preparation of the programs, all fall to the director and School of Theatre staff. With these managerial functions, academia's "producer-directors" also serve as teacher-professors, giving students both theoretical and practical experience through classes and play-production workshops. The academic "producer-director" must shrewdly ascertain what level of drama the student-actors can achieve—with their instructors' experienced tutoring—before an appropriate vehicle can be selected, interpreted, rehearsed, and moved to the university stage and audience.

Theatre studies from mid-century to the present have demonstrated that whether a commercial, regional, or academic venue generated a production, clear lines of authority and full communication between producer and theatre team were imperative to success. These studies show that a weakness in communication and interaction often lowers the quality of the performance itself, whereas the opposite—a smooth collaboration by the theatre team—virtually ensures a fine movement of script to audience. Whether theatre groups opt to develop a work from a legitimate or a musical theatre category, their selection may require a search through an imposing body of drama. The ultimate decision of genre and style rests with the sponsoring group's taste, purpose, and pocketbook. The proposed site and the current fashion are also factors—with the latter the least constant.

Producers who choose either legitimate or musical theatre might deplore some of the lighter fare that today lights up Broadway, calling it "spectacle," not drama—an esape from life rather than an involvement in it. Yet laments about the present trends in theatre need not quell enthusiasm: Continuity in dramatic content or style has not been an absolute on the theatre stages of the West. Instead, cyclical movement has flourished, to the credit of wise and patient production teams. Over centuries, the choices of our theatre groups have led them to advance or to retreat rather than stay with the status quo in content or style. Whether a particular group's preference was to tackle the untried or to recoup the past, the prevailing mode in the history of playscript and performance has been one of change—a challenging of accepted patterns in all types of theatre, whether nonmusical or musical. To choose a vehicle for staging from today's available styles and genres, the producer needs a rudimentary acquaintance with the development of drama from past to present forms.

LEGITIMATE THEATRE

With production teams' steady urge for innovation, the body of drama commonly called "legitimate theatre" has expanded through centuries, from Greek and Roman festivals' lyric-drama to medieval dramatizations of liturgy in miracle and saints plays; from Renaissance court comedies, tragedies, social satires, and chronicle history plays to Restoration comedies of manner and heroic plays (Thrall, Hibbard, and Holman 1960, 151). By the nineteenth century, though melodrama reigned, it coexisted with realistic problem plays and domestic tragedies until the twentieth century opted for naturalism, theatricality, or the "absurd" on its stages (Thrall, Hibbard, and Holman 1960, 153). Contemporary authors are further widening producers' choices with problem or situation plays that focus on dialogue and idea as much as on spectacle and scenic display. When today's commercial producers contemplate production, they cope with this residual mass of content and style. Theatre teams in our regional or repertory theatres and in University Schools of Theatre watch a long-run, passing-show of credo and custom. This bully audience constantly assesses the current mode in drama, noting whether it moves toward or away from naturalism, favors or opposes lavish display, chooses or disdains action-packed plots. Their concern is to appraise the multiplicity of form and the innovative styles of presenting it, and to decide whether a present, past, or previously untried mode most closely fits the group's own intent for theatre.

Each theatre group's particular intent or objective may differ from that of other units, yet for each to state its purpose will be possible if its members are in accord on their specific *raison d'être*. A consensus on the unit's rationale for approaching an audience—whether to startle and awaken, to inform or reform, to arouse remorse or pride—will help the group narrow its choices on the nature of the vehicle to be produced and the style with which to present it. In earlier ages, the rationale for engaging in drama "circled between a primitive wish to bask in fertility rites and sexuality or a more decorous toying with philosophical and spiritual themes" (Brockett 1982, 6). Also much enjoyed were countless types of comedy, specifically labeled "gross," "joyous," "bitter," or "tragic"; forms of tragedy called "poetic," "domestic," "heroic"; and styles of romance—"serene," "melodramatic," "fantastic" (Brockett 1982, 6). Length of drama was also varied, from the classic three- to five-act play to the more recent short play. Even drama's inner emphases were diverse, ranging between plays stressing spectacle, action, or scenery to those treating ideas and situations (Thrall, Hibbard, and Holman 1960, 152). Combinations of form and style lent engaging variety to production. Today's theatre professionals, contemplating this mass (or glut) of possibilities, are choosing what suits their objective.

Another matter of choice for today's producers and their teams has surfaced from the wide variety of facilities available for housing and staging a playscript today. In early theatre, performers used stalls, street corners, or churches as places for performance. In later periods, movable, outdoor stages appeared at festivals and forums; huge theatres with proscenium and thrust stages subsequently arrived (Thrall, Hibbard, and Holman 1960, 526). More recently, however, theatre again is often housed in smaller spaces, with arena stages whose atmosphere lends intimacy between audience and actors. With this range of facilities, today's producers can choose an appropriate venue for scripts that flaunt spectacle and action or for those that stress idea and situation.

Similar fluctuations have brought adjustments in the producer's authority over text and responsibility to its playwright. In some decades, a playwright's script functioned as "source" of artistic interpretation, with the playwright often in attendance throughout rehearsals. The producer, as a rule, served as financial and managing entity, less often as an active player in interpretation and rehearsal of the playscript. In other decades, the director controlled all aspects of performance, interpreting the script and guiding it through rehearsals. However, deviations from such presumptive patterns and their distinct poles of action have always been present, with the definition of roles ranging back and forth between separation and overlapping of functions. This evolution in the functions of producer, playwright, and director, like the shifting in drama's form and style, has been neither constant nor evenly paced.

Today's theatre teams seem increasingly aware that communication and interaction can curb or lessen overlaps in authority and responsibility. Conflicts may still surface from held-over views of role and function, as well as in choices of genre and style; yet the process of resolving discord may, of itself, launch fresh approaches to production.

MUSICAL THEATRE

Producers who wish to add musical theatre to their season will not need a vast infrastructure with which to prepare a score. They will need, however, a facility with sufficient space in which to prepare and present a musical score. Harmony will result if the producer, before choosing a specific piece of theatre, considers several requisites for musical theatre: an adequate physical facility, available fiscal support for the project, requisite skills and techniques of the actors, and accessible professional staff for the development of the score.

The size of the stage and the acoustics of the hall must accommodate the score's musical numbers. Producers will need to provide sufficient rehearsal time and space in which singers and dancers can master the complexities of the genre's libretto, songs, and lyrics. The management's budget must stretch to cover proposed expenses. (With musicals like *Fiddler on the Roof*, whose legal contract requires a producer to adhere to the score's original staging, such restrictions may exceed what is practical and necessary.)

Because the content of today's musicals often focuses on characterization and conflict as well as on song and dance, the producer's concern will also lie with the acting artistry of the singers and dancers selected to interpret the verbal passages of the play. As actors, the singer-dancers may require special coaching to make use of physical, emotional, and vocal systems that enhance actors' breathing, projection, and intelligibility in performance.

Although commercial venues often hire an artistic and a music director as well as a choreographer to develop a show's book, lyrics, and music, a simpler staffing can suffice at regional and academic venues. A pianist and an offstage piano can replace an orchestra; carefully selected actors may obviate the need for professional acting or vocal coaches. Experienced directors can build confidence in actors who approach musicals as a new field, one in which they will sing and/or dance as well as speak. The actors already possess these basic talents when they obtain their roles; the rehearsal experience lets them note the reaction of directors and other actors to their interpretation and delivery of the spoken text. Rehearsal also helps them acquire confidence enough to become judges of their own work. Singers and dancers who can stretch their performance skills to include artistic delivery of speaking parts will help audiences appreciate the worth and sophistication of today's musical scripts and scores. With experience, many find the singing of a lyric's verse and chorus as rewarding as delivering a soliloquy in a nonmusical drama (David Craig 1978, xxii).

Musical theatre producers have a gradually expanding body of drama from which to choose. From an age-old type of theatre, musicals have evolved into an acknowledged artistic form. Choral and instrumental music accompanied performance from the outset, from ritual dancing to court ballets. In medieval periods, music served a vital part in festivals and religious rites. For centuries, opera formed the mainstay of musical performance in Europe. In the 1860s, light operettas became popular on America's Broadway, imported from England, France, and Vienna. From them, a less traditional form unfolded here—a comedy with music. By the turn of the century, the form had evolved into a popular pastiche by composers like Victor Herbert and Jerome Kern (Engel 1977, xii). The earliest shows were not librettos with songs and lyrics but revues—collections of individual songs, often unrelated to characters or situations. Their lyrics dealt with old-hat subjects, and staging showed little originality of concept and execution. Early ones were billed as "Vanities" or "Follies," razzmatazz performances of dance and song; their librettos served only as links between the songs and dances (Engel 1977, 73). Their content was sparse, their characterization flat. Their writers used adolescent plots with girls-for-girls-sake staging (Engel 1977, xiv). From these came burlesque, pantomime, and vaudeville. Jerome Kern's *Girl from Utah* (1914) was typical of these highly popular shows, whose titles were often simplistic and indicative of content—for example, 1920's *Say Mama* and *Jazz à la Carte*; 1928's *Me For You* and *She's My Baby*.

Notable improvements appeared in the genre a few decades later when the song and dance shows developed plot lines and emphasized ideas and satires more than "girls" (Engel 1977, xv). By the late 1930s, the form had librettos with less-predictable plots and with better-developed characters, and huge choruses and dance spectacles were cut. At this point, the form was called "musical theatre" rather than "musical show" or "musical comedy" (Gordon Craig 1956, 100).

With today's inflated economics, productions are often unvarnished and simple, with costs of production lessened from earlier years. Lighting can limit or expand a staging area; furniture and props can be less than representative. Movable arches and plastic forms are shifted across the stage to indicate walls and furniture. The present store of new musicals, however, is insufficient for today's growing audience for musical theatre; revivals of the old, spectacular pieces still flood theatres on America's Broadway and London's West End, though simpler productions are also present. Opportunity is rife for new pieces of musical theatre. On Broadway in 1996, new librettos numbered nine, and the revivals of old ones numbered eleven (*Playbill*, June 1997). In England, musicals—many of them revivals—occupied twenty-one of the thirty-five central London playhouses, and "more are on the way" (Morley 1995, 26). Patrons of London's West End awaited the transfer of an old classic, Harold Prince's production of *Showboat*, a revival of Jerome Kern and Oscar Hammerstein's early musical for which Prince recently won his twentieth Tony.

In February 1996, the English eagerly welcomed a more recent hit, Broadway's *The Who's Tommy*, to their Shaftesbury Theatre.

Our producers and their staffs recognize that musical theatre, like nonmusical, has the capacity to reach diverse sections of theatregoers by its approach to serious issues of existence. As theatre history has shown, "One *Three-Penny Opera* sings all we have to know about man's inhumanity to man" (Gordon Craig 1956, 252) by its attention to those issues. To maintain the quality of the genre, today's theatre producers can search out the freshest pieces of musical theatre and avoid revivals of splashy song-and-dance vehicles or hollow old shows with "nothing to say/or sing in anything approaching a voice" (Gordon Craig 1956, 252). To increase our stock of new musicals and to lower the cost of producing them, our theatre teams can experiment with simpler content and techniques in our more-modest regional and academic venues. Old assumptions that musical theatre requires full choruses of dancing and singing actors can be discarded. What is vital is to encourage those who enter the musical theatre arena to prepare themselves for roles that encompass not only singing and dancing but also skillful acting. Actors with this measure of skill will encourage producers and their teams to meet the growing appetite of today's audiences for significant musical theatre. When a producer's care ensures the space and personnel that can move the script's music, design, and choreography to the stage, the result can be consummate theatre. Across the footlights, today's audiences are recognizing that both musical and nonmusical theatre offer dramatic experiences. Behind the footlights, our actors are realizing that success in musical theatre can give them self-esteem and acclaim in their careers (David Craig 1978, xxii).

2

Interviews, Personal Accounts, Comments by Producers

In literate, firsthand accounts by producers lie clues to the complexity of taking a script to the stage. In the specific interviews that follow, the comments by the organizers of New York City's Signature Theatre Company give us a valuable record of one team's interaction to fulfill their audiences' aspirations for dynamic theatre. With production heads delineating their lines of authority as precisely as those at the Signature Company, the audience has grown steadily.

Interview with James Houghton, Producer and Artistic Director of the Signature Theatre Company, New York, New York

This interview and the one that follows with Thomas Proehl were conducted by Susan Johann, professional photographer and writer, New York, 1996. Johann is company photographer for the group. Her photos and interviews with many of today's theatre figures are seen in national magazines and newspapers.

James Houghton: I started the Signature Theatre Company five seasons ago because I felt that playwrights were not involved in the staging process, nor truly welcomed into it.

To me, there's something very backward about that. I feel that if we had the opportunity to have [Anton] Chekhov in the room, everyone would jump at that opportunity. So why not have these writers in the room now? I'm not saying every writer is a Chekhov, but why not take that opportunity and not be frightened by it? Some producers and directors seem intimidated by writers. Yet I have found the playwrights I've worked with to be generous and open once they realize they are in a trusting environment rather than one that gives them only lip service or a bogus mission. If they feel truly invited in, then I find they completely open up to ideas, to directors and actors.

Susan Johann: When you started the Signature Group, did you envision that it would continue for more than a season?

James Houghton: I had the idea for the first season when I was attending an after-opening outing with friends. Romulus Linney was there. Many of us who had worked with Romulus thought him a tremendous writer and wanted to work with him again. I had this thought: We could do a whole season of Romulus, whose work was broad in scope and quite diverse. When Romulus left the room, I suggested to the group that we should try to organize all the people who supported him. A good friend called me two weeks later; he had remembered my idea when he stumbled upon a theatre space (the Kampo Culture Center [Manhattan]). We convinced the owner to rent the space to us for a year to try this concept of a season of one writer. So Romulus and I sat down together to figure out a season, then went forward on it.

I started a theater company with a particular mission, which wasn't just Romulus's mission but one that went way beyond this one writer. I realized that this concept of an examination of one writer's work might be welcomed by many writers. Then I set the Signature up so that it would be a long-term thing. It has worked well.

Susan Johann: In that first season, you managed the group alone?

James Houghton: There were other people there, but I was ultimately responsible for every aspect. I am still responsible, but the difference is that I have good, trusting people to whom I have delegated many of the job responsibilities. I have handed the production functions over to Elliot Fox; I don't have to be at the theater for every single rehearsal anymore. Elliot goes in, loads the set in, and he and I are in close contact the whole time. Tom Proehl, who is the managing director, takes care of everything financial. He and I go over all budgets together, though Tom does every bit of the work of balancing the books. That frees me to deal with the quality—the artistic quality—of the production and directing.

We're just at the tail end of the Adrienne Kennedy season. I have the Sam Shepard season coming up—have been into it for two or three months. And I'm into the season following. I'm talking to several writers now for the season after Sam, and writing a few people about the season after that. I have to be far ahead of the ball game.

As we have grown, our funding issues have become pressing. In the company's first year, the figures were much smaller in terms of budget. But as the figures grow, we have to find different sources to raise that kind of money. We have to know what we're doing further in advance in order to compete for grants. I need to decide what artistic programs we will select for our company. We are also in the middle of setting up a capital campaign. We want either to build a theatre or to take an existing space and renovate it. We are constantly developing.

By setting up the company as I did, with one season to a writer, I want the playwrights to have a place they can truly call their home-for-a-year. A sense of commitment and trust develops during the year, in contrast to the initial awkwardness of a single play, where a playwright meets for the first time with the designers and actors. In the latter situation, each one is spending three-quarters of his time trying to figure out what his relationship is to be with each person, as opposed to addressing the work itself. In our setup, we get through that awkward time almost immediately. For a writer to commit to the theatre for an entire year is an enormous decision for him and for the theatre group. We think long and hard before making that kind of decision. It takes energy and courage to agree to put oneself out there that many times in a climate like New York City.

Susan Johann: How active are you in the production process?

James Houghton: I have a design team—five designers in residence. Two costume designers have worked as a team for quite a few of the shows, Theresa Snyder-Stein and Jonathan Green. David Kosier is our set designer; Jeffrey Koger our lighting designer; and Jim van Bergen, whom I added just this year, is our sound designer. These are all people I had worked with, whom I've known for a long time; they truly listen to the playwright and incorporate his work into the design. I think writers often feel not threatened but disappointed in designers because they feel that the designs can overwhelm a play. I think they often do. So we always try to work from the playwright's word first. That's the general notion of our theatre, anyway. Since my designers will all have been there from the outset, the writers can develop a relationship with them, know their work, how they work, and vice versa. After their experience at Signature, most of our playwrights will use these designers again.

Susan Johann: Do you find yourself involved in casting, or is it handled primarily by the director?

James Houghton: I am involved in every aspect of the artistic process. Typically we have a casting director, Jerry Beaver, who has done a terrific job for us. Jerry, the director, and I talk, and between us Jerry comes up with a breakdown of the play's characters that we can discuss. We all have equal input. Jerry gets submissions from agents all over town; he also asks me, the director, and the playwright about anyone we might have in mind. We assemble several days of auditions on the basis of submissions selected by Jerry and all of us. In some cases I won't be at the general audition; however, I always attend the callback audition. Often I attend both.

Susan Johann: If two or three of the staff choose one actor but others are not in agreement, do you step in at that point?

James Houghton: If I had to, I would, but it has not happened. Almost always the playwright will attend the callback session as well. On a number of occasions, director or playwright has liked someone, and their number-one choice is my number-two choice. I've always gone with them because my number-two choice is still an excellent actor. I'm not directing the play; if I were, then that would be a different story. I'm working with people who have been making casting choices for a long time. And I generally find the casting process extremely illuminating, particularly when the writer is involved. It gives me such clarity when I watch a writer observe the actors walking through the door. I get a sense of where this writer is coming from, and I understand more about the character now because the writer is sort of clarifying the role through the casting process. More often than not, the director, writer, and I are all in line.

Susan Johann: Your scenic design and costume design are handled similarly?

James Houghton: Again, the writer is involved in the process from the start, as is the director. We meet together, have production meetings where we discuss design concepts and costumes. I've been a director, and generally my directors are not people who are working for the first time with the writer. I have conferred with the writer at the beginning of the year; we have talked about the plays and about possible directors. For instance, with Sam Shepard next year [1997], Joe Chaikin will be directing. Joe and Sam have known each other for thirty-some years. Sam has an inherent trust in Joe and vice versa; they know things about one another that no one else knows, and their relationship is completely unique. That brings strength to production; it keeps it on such a strong footing that divisive issues don't often come up. Now, if I threw a brand-new, cold director at Sam Shepard or Adrienne Kennedy or Edward Albee, there's a likelihood that those issues might arise. But because I am working with the writer generally for a year before we ever get to production, the relationship develops and I have a clear understanding of what the writer, director, designer, and actors are looking for. My job is to assemble them all and create an environment where creativity can happen.

Susan Johann: How much does budget affect that environment?

James Houghton: Budget affects us in that we can afford to pay actors only so much, can afford so much for the set, and must make choices.

We are in a larger space now, twice the size, twice the money. However, I always tell the designer, playwright, and director that I don't like to see them limit themselves because of budget. I say, "Let's pretend there isn't a budget; what would be ideal for this space and this play?" And almost always we're able to do it. Only on one occasion in the five years have I felt we could not. Our facility didn't make it possible. It was for a production of Edward Albee's play *Box*, where we tried to create a contraption (a steel-frame box) that could disappear in a minute. We could have done it if we had a fly system available. It was an evening of three one-act plays, making it essential that the operation of the box be smooth. We did not want to stop the progress of the play for the box to be broken down. Ultimately we all came to the decision that we just could not do it. We looked into the expense of designing some intricate box that collapsed and went up, but it did not make any sense. That's the only time I can think of where we didn't do something because we were limited by space or money. My whole concept is to present our plays in a manner that the playwright can feel proud of, can feel that the staging is accurate and that it captures at least part of his initial impulse for character, play, and story. My goal is to present a performance that the playwright can't walk away from saying, "I didn't like the production." It is important to me; it is essential. At other venues, playwrights may have a whole, huge, fully-budgeted production; yet when they see it, they feel that it barely resembles their play. We hope that does not happen at Signature. It is what we're attempting to prevent.

Susan Johann: Could you comment on the differences between staging a new play and a revival?

James Houghton: In one sense, the difference is great; in another, there is none. While we may do a play that has been done before, we never do a revival for the sake of a revival—a remounting of a play. As we consider these plays and put the season together, we always have a very good reason behind every production we choose. In the Lee Blessing season, *Two Rooms* had been done all over the country but never in New York. Hence ours was the play's New York premiere. There's a certain edge to that, a need to present it as clearly as possible at its New York premiere. In a play like Albee's *Sand Box*, one that's been produced before in New York, we made it part of an evening that, as an evening, had never been presented before. That production of *Sand Box*, I think, is among the best work we've done in our five years. Perhaps a previous production of it had fully satisfied the playwright, yet we're trying to take that memory away and create a new memory. In the Adrienne Kennedy season, she had previously had a wonderful production of *Funnyhouse of the Negro* (1964), but she had a lot of negative memories tied to it because of it closing early. We took the production, remounted it, had packed houses and an unbelievable run. Now she has a new memory tied to that piece. We helped alleviate the bad elements of the old, but kept the good ones. We stay away from revivals for the sake of revival. With each writer, we could have done a *Virginia Woolf*. In fact, in Edward Albee's season, we talked of staging *Zoo Story*. We were planning a production of two one-acts, *Counting The Ways* and *Listening*. *Listening* is a very difficult piece that both Edward and I were a little hesitant about, aware that it is not his most accessible play. Edward suggested that perhaps we should do *Zoo Story*. In that moment I thought how thrilling it would be to stage it, especially with the playwright himself directing it. Yet I knew that what we needed to present was *Listening*, the play that had not been seen, the one we were most worried about. That's the play we produced. And that has been my general philosophy behind the company. I want to broaden the position of these writers and inspire an audience's appreciation for them.

Susan Johann: What was your rationale for selecting *Young Man from Atlanta*?

James Houghton: In terms of *Young Man*, there's always an excitement with a new play. We actually did two premieres that year, world premieres, of Horton's [Foote]. With a world premiere, we had that first-time experience that you can't beat. It's developing character for the first time; it's the first time the playwright really experiences his characters on stage, filled with the minds and voices of actors. Each staging can change and evolve a play. We always try to throw the premieres toward the end of the season. By then, we all know and trust each other so well that an environment for creativity exists. That atmosphere displaces the uneasy one that often arises at a one-shot production.

Working on a new piece is exciting because the playwright is often in the rehearsal room, rewriting lines as we go. Horton may step out for a few minutes and rewrite a quick couple of passages to make something clearer. The actor may bring up a point that the playwright had not realized was unclear. Both the collaboration and the sense of exchange are thrilling. I think we have it throughout the season; yet it is definitely enhanced on a new piece. New pieces are tough in that we have only the same amount of rehearsal time—four weeks. We need a little more time for a new, raw piece.

Susan Johann: Do you use the same rehearsal space for each production?

James Houghton: It depends on availability and on need. For some productions we have thirteen actors, and for some only four. Since space is extremely expensive in New York, we try to be as creative with it as possible. We are renting the Shiva Theater from the public for the full nine- or ten-month season. We have altered it, doubling the rake of the risers. Now the dynamic makes the audience feel much more *in* it as opposed to observing it; that's always important to me. The rake in the house is now very severe, going right down to floor level. I like that dynamic. Acoustically I think it's probably their best space. I like the size. We had certain challenges there from pillars that are part of the old library. We worked around them and achieved more depth for the stage. With this season I knew we would use multimedia, for which we would need this depth. We don't rent rehearsal space there, though, only the theater. We're in the middle of trying to find a new space. We have to find a theater by '97–'98.

Susan Johann: You have a four-week rehearsal period no matter what?

James Houghton: That's Actors Equity. If it's a musical, we can have five weeks. I would like more rehearsal, but we can't have more. It's a union thing. On a Letter of Agreement, we are allowed only four weeks of rehearsal. One advantage for us is that we have a theatre that's a reasonable size, with economics that are reasonable. If I had a steady flow of money, I could operate differently; but that's not reality. I don't want economics to dictate artistic policy. I don't want to start thinking, "I'd better not do that writer" or "We can't do that play." We've opted for some very difficult material from major writers, work that is noncommercial and underproduced. Again, these are works that most groups would not produce. We're able to choose this material because we're producing a whole body of one writer's work. Our mission is not to be a full, commercial theatre. That's not what we're about. I want to have a larger theatre, to have several spaces; yet I always want the economics to be in favor of the artistic policy.

Susan Johann: It's your vision that drives your mission?

James Houghton: Absolutely. It's everything. Without the mission it's just another production. To me, our mission is the larger picture, not any one production. *Young Man from Atlanta* won the Pulitzer; yet that season was not about *Young Man from Atlanta*. The season was about Horton Foote and four incredible productions, representing a broad range of his work. The fact that audiences acknowledged that one particular play and the other plays to various degrees is great. But if we limit ourselves to that, then it's time for me to move on and for the company to fold. It cannot become that limited, or it will be just one more company.

Interview with Thomas Proehl, Producer/Managing Director of the Signature Theatre Company, New York, New York

Susan Johann: What does a managing director do?

Thomas Proehl: My position is very much involved with the business of production. All of the financial information of the company must go through me to be monitored. The company's artistic director, James

Houghton, decides what plays we will produce, and then it is my responsibility to find and manage the money to finance them. I negotiate
all contracts with the actors, with Actors Equity, with the designers, and
with the author. All of the office equipment has to be bought or leased.
I oversee everything that we need to keep the office operating and the
productions running.

I determine how much money we have; then Elliot Fox, our associate
director, secures the production designs from the designer and orders
the supplies to build them. If we need more for costumes, we borrow
from the set's budget line. If we need more for lighting, we borrow from
other budget lines. Basically it is a juggling act to come out on the bottom
line.

Susan Johann: How is it different from being Chief Financial Officer?

Thomas Proehl: We are a not-for-profit organization. Our investment is
the production. In a nonprofit situation like ours, my position is listed
as all-encompassing managing director. Some of the larger institutions
do have a finance officer, a controller, and an accountant. Here, I do all
the bookkeeping, accounting, and financial statements. Then I turn my
books over to an auditor once a year.

Susan Johann: How well had your prior training and experience prepared you for this position?

Thomas Proehl: My undergraduate degree was in acting and directing
with a double major in accounting. Then I followed a Masters program
in Arts Administration. For eight years I was general manager at the
Dramatists' Guild.

Susan Johann: Do you feel immersed in computers for your accounting?

Thomas Proehl: We are desperately behind in technology at Signature
because we cannot yet afford the new programs we hope to have soon.
We want to get online, to be able to surf the Net. We want to be able to
create information in-house networks so that we're sharing information.
The biggest problem is getting machines that are capable of being up-
graded and software that is top of the line. We must keep up with the
currents; marketing, especially for theatre, has to change. Much of it must
go to the Internet, a different world.

Susan Johann: How much are you involved in production?

Thomas Proehl: I'm not a Broadway producer who has a huge production office, who goes out to find money from backers. For my purposes,
I will always be nonprofit because for us, the institution comes first. It
survives from year to year. With Broadway theatre organizations, the
play is King, and when the play loses, nothing is left. Here, we invest
our time and our efforts into this institution, creating a larger body of
work than one play. The season may end, but the institution goes on.

Susan Johann: What is your function in raising money?

Thomas Proehl: In the budgeting process, we work with the expense side first. We determine our needs for the plays to be produced. Then we approach the other side: How many subscriptions can we sell, and how many single tickets? Then we consider what other revenue sources we can have; parking may be one in the future. We look at possibilities, make an educated guess based on what we can do now. To be over-zealous on the earned income is foolhardy. By estimating our costs less the earned revenue, we come up with a total deficit to be funded. Then we decide where we are to get the money. Most of it is individual or foundation giving; each year we have to create a bigger picture, a broader exposure for our name. It is all about selling ourselves.

Susan Johann: Your budget has changed significantly in the last five years?

Thomas Proehl: The first year was $34,000 for four plays. That was the Romulus Linney season. The next year it was $43,000 for the Lee Blessing season.

Susan Johann: And these were seasons that received major reviews. Lee Blessing's play was mentioned in *Time* magazine as one of the year's ten best!

Thomas Proehl: Right. The [Edward] Albee season was number three, with a budget of $108,000. The Horton Foote season had a $200,000 budget, and the Adrienne Kennedy season was $475,000. The rise comes because we now have a staff, which we did not have before. We are paying people instead of using volunteers. We are paying for our sets now. Since the total square footage of the Shiva Theatre is much larger than our first space, the sets have become larger. Our actors must now be Equity; their salaries have gone up, and they get pension and health benefits. With these greater expenses, our budget may reach $1,000,000 next year. Equity is a huge expense; in this year's Letter of Agreement, we had a waiver giving us four rehearsal weeks on a reimbursement, with the performance weeks on contract. Next year everyone is on contract from day one, and we'll have six-week runs. We anticipate huge increases in subscribers; we hope to fill four weeks with subscribers and then have two weeks to sell single tickets. Most of the increased expense comes with the larger size of production in our new space. We will also have a coproduction with Second Stage, with whom we'll stage *Tooth of Crime*, a huge undertaking. We are planning for the most exposure and hoping it will be a real blast.

Susan Johann: If a play goes on to another venue after you produce it, as *Young Man from Atlanta* did, how does that production figure into the financial contract?

Thomas Proehl: We share in a very small portion of the original plays that we produce. For anything that's been produced before, the subsid-iary rights have been exploited already, so we don't share in those. If we move a play in the city as a direct result of our staging, and if it is our production (i.e., at least half of the cast, the same director and designers), then that is a negotiated point wherein we receive a portion of the box office from that play for its New York run. But for *Young Man from Atlanta*, for instance, we shared only in a portion, a very small percentage of the author's share, diluted so many times that it is nothing one can bank on. We can make money on the subsidiary rights only if the play sells as a movie or goes to Broadway—and runs fifteen years!

Susan Johann: Can you think of other points related to your work on a day-to-day basis?

Thomas Proehl: First I return the many phone calls that have come in through the night. My routine is ongoing each season: At this time, we are in the budgeting process for next year [1997]; when we are in production, I am working with sales and tickets. In addition, as company manager, I go to the theatre to work with actors, making sure they are happy, seeing that they are paid. My functions change, depending upon where we are in the year and on what needs to be done. Three of us take care of responsibilities in the office.

Susan Johann: On that nuts-and-bolts side, what kind of accounting software do you use?

Thomas Proehl: Right now I am using AccPac Plus, a very labor-intensive package. But now that we're expanding, I want to have a more efficient method. We have Database, d-Base IV software to maintain our mailing list—a huge job since people move around in New York City all the time. We use WordPerfect's basic standard software. We have recently applied for a grant that will streamline our whole system and put us into a development and box office system so that we can handle our own season tickets. My job is to watch the cash flow—particularly flowing out. But when the cash flows in, it is great!

3

The Producer's Interaction with the Theatre Team in Legitimate Theatre

In theatre lore, smooth interaction between a producer and other members of the production team has long been held essential. By the mid-twentieth century, however, less-than-total harmony often marred productions. Some teams lacked accord on what would or would not move a play from working script to artistic performance.

A troublesome concept needed severe testing—the notion that a producer was a figure who put up the money for production then stepped back to await the profits. Even such a limiting definition of a producer as one made facetiously by director Alan Schneider allowed the figure to stay somewhat involved after the check was written: "A good producer is not only the person who has the good taste to hire you and never reminds you of this at the wrong time, but also someone who's there when you need him and who stays away when you don't" (Schneider 1986, 103). Producers had been seeking a more integral slot in the artistic side of production, choosing actors and designers, taking part in the text's interpretation and rehearsal. When producers opted to assume these functions rather than remain in outer-management circles, difficulties easily arose. Yet when lines of authority and responsibility between producer and director were more precisely delineated, the results more adequately filled the expectations of theatre teams and their audiences.

MID-TWENTIETH CENTURY PRODUCERS

Three theatre teams in the 1940s and 1950s demonstrated particularly disparate patterns of interaction and strikingly diverse results in their staging of three unique playscripts. The first instance involved producer Nat Karson, the second, producer Robert Whitehead, and the third, producer Michael Myerberg. Each of the three worked with the same director, a now legendary and acclaimed figure, Alan Schneider.

In 1948, the work of the first pair, producer Nat Karson and director Alan Schneider, displayed less-than-smooth interaction staging *A Long Way from Home* (an adaptation of Maxim Gorki's *Lower Depths*), though the audiences received the production well. Fortunately, the 1953 involvement of producer Robert Whitehead and director Alan Schneider in Liam O'Brien's *The Remarkable Mr. Pennypacker* was remarkably harmonious and the production completely successful. The 1956 partnership of producer Michael Myerberg and director Alan Schneider, however, on Samuel Beckett's *Waiting for Godot*, encountered such striking disagreement and hostility that the marred production still looms ubiquitously in theatre history's annals. (N.B.: Schneider, working with other producers later, directed the same Beckett play to monumental acclaim.) Understandably, Schneider, in his autobiography, *Entrances*, called Karson and Myerberg "the exact opposites" of what he wanted in a producer, and he labeled Robert Whitehead "a good one" (along with Richard Barr and Zelda Fichandler). The latter three producers are remembered today as topflight production figures (Schneider 1986, 103).

Nat Karson and Alan Schneider: *A Long Way from Home*, 1948 (An Adaptation of Maxim Gorki's *Lower Depths*)

Of the Karson-Schneider relationship while preparing *A Long Way from Home* for the Maxine Elliott Theatre in New York City in February 1948, Schneider (1986) wrote, "[Karson] had never wanted to hire me and did so only under great pressure. He was never there when I needed him and always came around when I didn't want him" (103).

In the third week of rehearsals, Schneider, the actors, and the playwright (Randy Goodman) decided they "could survive a run-through for the big brass" (105). They announced the time, and the producer agreed to attend. Karson arrived as the rehearsal started. Schneider writes, "Nat walked in . . . sat, stony-faced and alone, through what the rest of us thought was a very exciting first viewing of the overall play. The actors were excited, the playwright [Randy Goodman] ecstatic. I was pleased. Randy and I turned eagerly to Nat for his reaction" (105). Surprise and bewilderment came when Karson reacted with immediacy: "I'm taking over." Stunned, Schneider asked, "What's wrong?" Karson answered that their work "was all wrong" and that he was going to "take over." (106). Goodman, too, was appalled; he insisted that he both liked and approved of what he himself had just seen (106). But Karson informed him that his opinion didn't matter, saying, "The producer is taking over."

Schneider later recalled, "That was my first experience with a phrase I was to hear many times in subsequent years" (105–6).

For the time being, however, without explanation, Karson seemed to back down—until the final week of rehearsals. During that week, Schneider, needing to approve the publicity proofs for the final program, first saw (above the play's title and his own name) the credit line, "Nat Karson's Production of." He left the line where it was but corrected the wording to "Produced by Nat Karson," which was the customary attribution on earlier programs of the same series Karson was producing for the theatre (108). The incident seemed of little consequence, and a few days later, the final rehearsal was scheduled. However, at 2:30 A.M., Karson called to order Schneider, "Don't you come around to that theater tomorrow! . . . I mean it, you bastard" (108). The following afternoon, Schneider ignored the order and went to the rehearsal, the last before the play's opening. There he found that his agent, Miss Audrey Wood, had sent a message of support for him; he relaxed slightly at her promise that she "was not about to see someone else come in at the very last minute to claim credit for directing this show. If necessary, she was even capable of getting up on the stage before the entire audience and telling everyone exactly what had happened" (111).

Almost at once, Karson arrived at the rehearsal, and brushed past the building's entryway where Schneider stood. When Karson entered the building, what happened was a shock. With Schneider still outside, Karson placed the cast in a semicircle and announced that he was taking over the production. The cast's reaction was immediate; one by one they told the stage manager that they were ill, then exited and headed for an habitual gathering spot for them—a corner drugstore—calling to Schneider as they passed him on the sidewalk, "See ya down at the corner" (111). Schneider followed and joined the cast at the drugstore. After fifteen minutes, a puzzling note arrived for Schneider from Karson, saying "We're waiting for you. It's going to be a terrific show" (112). When the cast and director returned, Karson was sitting quietly, at the back of the auditorium on the far side. Schneider resumed his directing of the actors, and by the end of rehearsal, Karson had left the theatre.

At the opening, with no further intervention by the producer, the show "went unerringly well. . . . The ten daily critics came out in full force" (112). The *New York Times'* Brooks Atkinson wrote, "Under Alan Schneider's direction . . . the show is vivid and fascinating, and one more Experimental Theatre achievement"; and George Freedley, the *Telegraph's* critic and the New York Public Library's Theater Collection curator, felt that "the show was exciting theater . . . something of which the whole theater can be proud" (113). Both playwright Randy Goodman and director Alan Schneider were proud—and relieved.

Robert Whitehead and Alan Schneider: *The Remarkable Mr. Pennypacker*

Of a far smoother nature was the 1953 interaction between producer Robert Whitehead and director Alan Schneider for *The Remarkable Mr. Pennypacker*, written by Liam O'Brien. Schneider (1986) found Whitehead "one of the kindest men in the American theater" (167), one who advised and supported him during any and all staging disquiet.

The production's cast included Burgess Meredith, Martha Scott, and Una Merkel. Meredith and Scott had reputations of being difficult actors to work with, and gave Schneider "his worst experience to date with the extreme volatility of theatre relationships . . . and demonstrated the difficulty of steering a safe course between the playwright and the players" (174). Yet as conflicts arose during staging, Whitehead—at times quietly, at others, actively, fully supported Schneider.

During rehearsals, when Martha Scott became chagrined at Schneider's supposed slighting of her in blocking the play's scenes (his positioning of her less centrally in respect to other actors), her agent demanded that Scott be blocked center stage more often than the other stars. Schneider "fiddled with the staging, trying hard to serve the play," and, at the same time, meet Martha Scott's demands for equal prominence with other actors in his blocking of her (174). Unable to please the actress, Schneider at last suggested that she speak to Whitehead. She did. Whitehead, however, told Schneider to "go right on directing the play the way he saw fit, and let [Whitehead] deal with Martha" (175). With the producer's backing, no further problem with the actress or her agent resulted.

Smooth interaction appeared, too, when for legal reasons the original name of the play (*The Family Man*) had to be changed. At first, Schneider and the cast openly expressed their anxiety over the move, groaning at the switch of title and the advanced-publicity mix-up that would arise with the mid-production change. Still, they all used their ingenuity, considered many titles, and reconciled themselves to a final Whitehead choice of *The Remarkable Mr. Pennypacker* (176). In time, they even found the new name appropriately humorous for the character who had two wives and families concurrently without revealing his bigamy to either one (176).

A bigger problem arose concerning the play's difficult and yet unfinished third act, which playwright Liam O'Brien had been unable to tackle. To help, Schneider and Whitehead worked with him, "tendering ideas . . . in endless conversations all through rehearsals" (176). The three discussed and debated possible content for the final act while rehearsals of the first two acts proceeded, but no text was forthcoming. Whitehead and Schneider shared their worry with each other, then finally approached the author at his hotel, where they assumed he was finishing the script. They found him exhausted and depressed, still "totally without a third act—though it was to go into rehearsal the next morning" (177). Whitehead and Schneider talked with him about how they could help. Together, the three exchanged suggestions. To encourage O'Brien, the producer and director began to improvise a possible scene as the playwright watched; the two were "trying to suggest what Pa and Ma Pennypacker might say or do once she learned of the existence of another separate but equal spouse and family" (177). Heartened, O'Brien listened; as they talked, he typed as much of their spontaneous dialogue as he could. After Whitehead and Schneider left, O'Brien finished the third act within hours that same night, and it was, producer and director agreed, "not appreciably lower in quality than the other acts"—though it was, like most third acts, a little shorter (177).

At the play's tryouts in Philadelphia, its reviews were "uniformly favorable, the subscription audiences liking it hugely and spreading the word" (177). At its opening in New York at the Coronet Theatre (now the Eugene O'Neill), critic Atkinson called the play "uproarious . . . filled with tenderness and charm . . . a lusty show" (178).

Final evidence of the harmony between Whitehead and Schneider appeared later in the play's run when the management of the theatre facility unexpectedly and abruptly shifted its policy on admission prices and types of seating available. They installed "elaborate two-seater 'divans' out of the highly desirable first six rows of seats for the play . . . sold at much higher prices . . . only at the box office, no tickets being assigned to the ticket brokers" (181). At once, the brokers refused to advertise the show or to give clients information about the time and place of performance. When Whitehead and Schneider learned of the problem, they objected to the shift in policy and its probable effect on attendance. They "threatened retaliation—legal action." Though their intervention was unsuccessful at the time, with prolonged pressure by the producer and director, eventually the management removed the "divans" and returned to previous ticketing policy. As both Whitehead and Schneider had expected, the sale of tickets quickly recovered, and the play topped the financial expectations of the backers (181).

The successful teamwork of producer Robert Whitehead and director Alan Schneider is plain from the elated director's summary comment on the play's reception: "We were a 'smash' " (179).

Michael Myerberg and Alan Schneider: *Waiting for Godot*, 1956

Theatre reviews show no use of the phrase "a smash" to describe 1956's Michael Myerberg–Alan Schneider collaboration on Samuel Beckett's *Waiting for Godot*. During the preparation of the play for its audience, a dearth of harmony between producer and director led to an unfortunate choice of actors, a fuzzy determination of set design, and an inability to select an appropriate theatre to house the performance. Equally flawed by lack of consultation between Myerberg and Schneider was the misleading publicity in advance of the opening and the distribution of gate receipts during the run.

When Myerberg had first sought Schneider to direct the Beckett play for its Broadway debut, the apprehensive director had "responded only halfheartedly" (Schneider 1986, 221). He was skeptical, sensing that *Waiting for Godot* was a serious drama suited for a more intimate and cerebral audience than Broadway usually offered. The play features two characters waiting for someone to come with an answer to the meaning in their lives, but the promised and expected arrival never takes place (248). Schneider had seen the play in Paris at a tiny, Left Bank venue (Théâtre Babylone) two years before and was awed by Beckett's gift for language and rhythm, for "making the sublime ridiculous and the ridiculous sublime" (248). Myerberg insisted that *Waiting for Godot* was Broadway material and Broadway-bound; friends, however, having seen an early London production of the play, cautioned Myerberg that the work was "not really right for the American Theatre" (186). Representatives of the New York Press at the Paris and London staging had been "intrigued but baffled" by the "weird" play (186). At the London showing, Schneider had experienced the play as "something unique in modern theatre"—profound but far from the splendor and spectacle that Broadway demanded in its fare (186). He did not, therefore, deem Myerberg's plan for a Broadway showing appropriate for the play's initial American appearance. Schneider was also leery of any collaboration with Myerberg; he was aware that several contemporaries who had worked with the producer regarded him as a "devious and unreliable" figure, one whose productions were often bankrupt (117). Yet Schneider decided to accept Myerberg's proposal and proceed with the venture.

Rehearsals began within weeks, with the opening set for soon after Christmas at New York City's Music Box Theatre. What befell the play between rehearsals and opening confirms a long-acknowledged need for communication between producers and directors in production and for clear definition of responsibilities if a theatre team is to move a playscript to its audience successfully. Many years later, Schneider recalled that the complete failure of the production had led him at the time to resolve that for subsequent productions of any Beckett work that he might direct, no producer would ever again "get in the way of a proper presentation" (246).

Even before rehearsals, the grating failure of the Myerberg-Schneider venture had begun with a lack of discussion between the producer and his director over appropriate scenic design for the staging. Schneider had submitted to Myerberg a simple, carefully devised plan for the stage, one that Schneider and playwright Samuel Beckett had discussed at previous Paris and London meetings. Schneider's setting design was unobtrusive and in line with Beckett's long-time preference for bare lines and forms; the playwright considered all unnecessary display a distraction to audiences. Myerberg himself, however, wanted a far more elaborate set than Schneider had submitted. At Myerberg's request, his scenic designer devised one, which the producer instantly approved, instructing the designer not to tell the director until the revised set was constructed and in place. After Schneider saw the complicated, flashy setting and props, he was repulsed by its clutter, its lack of order. Yet it was too late for significant discussion with Myerberg on the design's unsuitability to Beckett's intent. Still, Schneider's reaction was so acute and obvious that, after weeks of argument, Myerberg directed his designer to remove some of the inappropriate clutter and restore a bit of the original, simple setting Schneider had submitted. Better initial communication between producer and director could have allayed the design crisis and eased the growing tension between producer and director.

Less easy to remedy were serious blunders in casting the play. From the outset, no collaboration had taken place between producer and director on actors who would play Beckett's leads or his other three characters. Before Schneider had signed on to direct, Myerberg had already hired two popular comedians, Bert Lahr and Tom Ewell, to play the two "top bananas," Estragon and Vladimir. For the remaining uncast roles of Pozzo, Lucky, and the Boy, Schneider suggested to Myerberg several actors whose work he knew and whose acting styles would fit Beckett's roles. At Schneider's meetings with Beckett in Paris, Schneider had studied the script thoroughly. He and Beckett had discussed Beckett's intentions for his characters while the two watched Peter Hall's London production of the play. Myerberg, however, ignored Schneider's counsel and hired actors on his own. Schneider was particularly dubious about Myerberg's selection of Jack Smart—a radio, TV, and film star—for the role of Pozzo, and equally skeptical of his choice of Charles Weidman—a dancer and choreographer with no acting experience—for the part of Lucky. Most disconcerting to Schneider was Myerberg's hiring of an older and equally inexperienced actor for the role of the Boy. As Schneider had feared, all five of Myerberg's choices suffered serious difficulties in finding their characters' natures and determining their importance to the play's through-line. Bert Lahr conceived his character, Estragon, to be the play's "top banana" and insisted that Tom Ewell (Vladimir) serve only as "a straight man who should be feeding Lahr's Estragon his laughs" (228). In contrast, Schneider saw both of the roles as "bananas," with Ewell's Vladimir actually "slightly more central to the play's thematic core" than Lahr's Estragon (228). With Lahr's concept of his character, however, he constantly ad-libbed, worked the audience, and delivered his role as he conceived it to be: part of a free and open vaude-ville sequence designed to draw uproarious laughs from viewers. The actor, dead-sure of his delivery, did not grasp the austere subtleties of Beckett's script (228). Myerberg, unfortunately, gave no support to his troubled director; throughout rehearsals, the producer encouraged Lahr with ready applause for what Schneider saw as his raucous and heartless delivery of the role. The other actors' problems arose, as Schneider had feared, from their total lack of experience in legitimate theatre. Schneider concentrated his efforts on leading the actors to a more sensitive percep-tion of Beckett's text, yet he could not lift their performance to a credible level before the opening.

Perhaps as damning to the premiere performance as the unstudied selection of the actors for Beckett's cast was the producer's midstream decision to book the production's tryouts into a splashy new facility near Miami, the Coral Gables Theatre. Its owners, seeking a comedy that could draw a crowd for their theatre's grand opening, had hoped to begin their season by engaging Marilyn Monroe in a glitzy comedy with Tom Ewell (who happened to be a friend of the theatre owners) as a droll backup to the actress. When the star, Monroe, proved unavailable, Myerberg—also a friend of the theatre owners—managed to convince them that his splendid project-in-progress, *Waiting for Godot*, starring popular vaude-ville star Bert Lahr and Tom Ewell, would be as terrific a draw as their first choice, Marilyn Monroe and company. Myerberg's carefully devised publicity in advance of the opening billed Beckett's serious, sublime drama as a riotous evening of laughs. His splashy publicity campaign beguiled and misled prospective audiences, whose anticipations were high—until they viewed the actual performance. Then, with their expec-tations dampened, the viewers' letdown was acute, their reaction negative and noisy, and the discerning press trashed the performance beyond Schneider's expectation.

Notwithstanding the disastrous critical and popular reaction to the play, Myerberg's strength of will kept it open briefly. As the rapport of producer and director worsened, Myerberg replaced Schneider with an-other director but refused to give Schneider his portion of whatever roy-alties had materialized. When Myerberg ended the play's short stay at Coral Gables, he opted to follow his earlier plan to take the production to New York; he hired yet another director and installed a far more experienced group of actors. With these improvements, the New York production was profitable enough that Myerberg eventually paid Schnei-der his long-delayed royalties from the Coral Gables fiasco.

Many producers, after Michael Myerberg's 1956 debacle with *Waiting for Godot*, mounted the Beckett play successfully. Producers Nina Vance, David Susskind, and Ely Landau developed the playscript with director

Alan Schneider for professional, regional, and academic producers, and for PBS television. With Nina Vance at the Alley Theatre in 1960, the performance was greeted favorably by critics and was received well by its audiences (266). Again, in 1960, David Susskind and Ely Landau produced *Waiting for Godot* for television's *Play-of-the-Week*. Though the work's thematic content was still termed "baffling" by some viewers, its staging was acclaimed as dramatic and moving. Other well-received productions of the play, with Schneider's enthusiastic direction, ran at New York City's Sheridan Square Playhouse, August 1971; at Stanford University's Theatre, August 1975; and at New York City's Public Theatre, April 1981.

Indexes and bibliographies in the field of drama hold comprehensive lists of noted producers who directed still other Beckett plays, some of them staged year after year at venues like New York City's Cherry Lane Theatre; Princeton's McCarter Theatre; Washington, D.C.'s Arena Stage; and New York City's East End Theatre. With the boost these producers gave to Beckett's reputation, many of his other dramas appeared repeatedly at regional and academic locations. Among those most often produced, and always directed by Alan Schneider, were: *Krapp's Last Tape* (six productions), *Happy Days* (three), *Ohio Impromptu* (three), *Footfalls* (three), *Rockaby* (five), *That Time* (five), *Endgame* (twice), *Not I* (twice), *Act without Words* (twice), *Catastrophe* (three), *What Where* (three), *Play* (three), *Come and Go* (twice), and *Breath* and *Eh Joe* (once).

Though the Myerberg–Schneider partnership on *Waiting for Godot* had drawn no bravos for the producer, these later, critically acclaimed Beckett productions earned the theatre world's top regard for American theatre producers and the respect and friendship of the play's author, Samuel Beckett. Printed mentions of Myerberg's collaborations with directors held less detail and appeared less often than those of producers Whitehead, Vance, Susskind, or Landau, whose harmonious production experiences kept their names on Broadway well into the 1980s.

THE 1990s: A PRODUCER WITH LONGEVITY: ROBERT WHITEHEAD

Producer Robert Whitehead, after four decades in the theatre, is still taking both new and established playwrights' works to Broadway. Two of these works, Arthur Miller's *Broken Glass* (1994) and Terrence McNally's *Master Class* (1996), have pulled critics' attention again toward Whitehead productions.

The reviews of the two plays were mixed; yet to base the status of long-time producers like Robert Whitehead solely on critics' estimates of selected stagings seems an invalid exercise. A truer estimate of our producer's career achievements should cover more than involvement in a specific production. It should be, at minimum, twofold, encompassing both production records and significant contributions to the nation's theatre, such as their organizational activities, forming of new groups, service on theatre committees, positions in national associations—functions that raise the level of our theatre yet may draw less public attention than the producers' ups and downs on Broadway.

The career of producer Robert Whitehead has been striking in both areas—level of production and amount of service. For his current swings on Broadway, his mounting of Arthur Miller's *Broken Glass* drew mixed reviews, whereas his staging of Terrence McNally's *Master Class* collected multiple bravos. To Whitehead's production of *Broken Glass*, a play that looks at a Jewish couple's symbiotic relationship of guilt and hostility, some critics gave their solid endorsement. Others dismissed the play as disappointing, though one critic focused not on his script but on its staging. John Lahr (1994) said, "It is a brave, big-hearted, compelling attempt, though not a particularly elegant one" (196). Robert Brustein (1994) objected that the Broadway production lacked dignity: "The British seem able to produce Miller with the grandeur of Shakespearean tragedy rather than (as here) with the prosaic flatness of a sociological primer" (29). Yet several critics called it "haunting and psychologically unsettling" though the production's scenic design was described as "lacklustre" and its structure as obviously sketchy and schematic (Lahr 1994, 196). Objections focused on production technique, referring to it as the "creaky machinery of *Broken Glass*" and citing its ill effect on the performance, making the play appear "very old-fashioned and clunky"; in fact, the production made the play appear "a shaky piece of stage architecture" (Brustein 1994, 30).

The play's casting itself may have lacked wisdom, because a very young and spirited actress, Amy Irving, played an older Jewish woman with a Brooklyn dialect who must sit in a wheelchair. Only the consummate skill of Amy Irving induced the audience to believe in her character's "compelling amalgam of regret and rage" and to accept its "calcifying effect" on her life and that of her husband (Lahr 1994, 95). The production's main distinction was that, with a paucity of "theatrical goings on" or dynamic stage business, it held its audience, with "nobody moving" (Lahr 1994, 96). Playwright Arthur Miller, highly pleased that the people in attendance listened with such complete attention, said of the production's success in absorbing viewers, "Now, you have to fight for that. You have to fight for that calm. That kind of reflectivity is dangerous in a theatre that is all hyped up, that thinks it cannot exist unless somebody is full of jokes or screaming or yelling" (quoted in Lahr 1994, 96).

In stark contrast to critics' reactions to Whitehead's *Broken Glass* production was their applause for McNally's *Master Class* (1996). Whitehead, whose wife, eminent actress Zoe Caldwell, played opera diva Maria Callas in *Master Class*, took the play on a pre–New York journey, beginning with a preview at the Philadelphia Theatre Company, then on to the Mark Taper Forum, Los Angeles, before it opened in New York in the fall of 1995. Whitehead had also produced *The Prime of Miss Jean Brodie* and directed another, *Medea*.

The production of *Master Class* brought high praise from critics for Whitehead's decision to back the show, for seeing the potential "body and heft" in an "essentially non-dramatic situation," then moving it to the stage in "a more than usually forceful tour de force" (Simon 1995, 88). Though one critic called the production "flashy" and "melodramatic" (Davis 1995, 89), most found it funny, touching, and accomplished. The two-act play's setting and decor, well-designed by Michael McGarty, was simple, containing a piano, a desk, and volumes of bound lyrics. It represented, at times, an auditorium, La Scala Opera House, a stage, and a rehearsal studio of Greek–American soprano Maria Callas, a "supreme musician" who gave her career away "in the name of love" (Haun 1995, 22). With shimmering lighting and swelling music, soliloquies at the end of each act become "dreamlike fantasies" with Callas (played by Zoe Caldwell) on a darkened stage, costumed in black (as was Callas's wont) often with only a spot of light on her face, reliving the highlights of her career (Hodgins 1995, 310). After abandoning the stage, Callas had once given master classes in a studio at Juilliard, where in the 1970s playwright Terrence McNally actually attended sessions taught by the opera diva.

The set's convoluted stage pieces were handled by Michael Friel, who moved them about "with the stolidity of an inveterate stagehand"; the lighting by Brian MacDevitt and costumes by Jane Greenwood were "impeccable" (Simon 1995, 88). Two flashbacks in the action were production standouts, each well focused on Callas's heady and involved personal life with her husband and her "high-profile affair" (Haun 1995, 22) with Aristotle Onassis. The set, through graphic projections, became an auditorium first and then a stage at La Scala, where Caldwell, in monodrama, revealed her love affairs to viewers. The play, however, was not a docudrama but a dynamic play with a "compelling exploration of the creative spirit" (Haun 1995, 20). The technique itself was striking, with the character "assuming the voices of the main men in her life" as she recalled their conversations (Simon 1995, 88). A wise production choice, too, was the use of an obsequious, onstage accompanist but with no actual singing by Caldwell—quite appropriate because at the time of Callas's master classes, her voice had deteriorated severely (Davis 1995, 89). The decision to waive the vocal score was wise; with the surfeit of musicals now on Broadway, Whitehead's lack of focus on Maria Callas as a "voice"—a figure consumed by music and singing—was "a step in the right direction" and a boon for audiences "starved for nonmusical theatre of merit" (Simon 1995, 89).

To these mixed critical assessments of recent Whitehead productions, one might well add a consideration of how fully and creatively this producer has functioned for decades in his theatre community, meeting broad and ongoing tugs at his organizational strengths. Producers of great worth to an era have exhibited, like Whitehead, a passion for theatre that led them to undertake additional activities associated with production. Typically, prominent production heads have included in their functions the forming of new repertory groups and the founding of production corporations (re: Whitehead's "Producers Theatre"), where producers and directors could reinforce a community's hopes to involve the public more fully in theatre. They have developed projects—Shakespeare festivals or children's theatre, activities that move producers up front at professional conferences and symposiums where they share their drive to renew theatre with their contemporaries. If a producer's rank in theatre is to be based upon these broad interests and activities as well as on a continuous flow of stagings to Broadway, the rating will seem valid.

Grounded upon these standards, Robert Whitehead has qualified for decades as a producer of excellence. During his career, he backed and managed a stream of productions that not only brought young, new actors into theatre but also furthered the careers of more-established artists—Ethel Barrymore, John Gielgud, Judith Anderson, Helen Hayes, Alfred Lunt, and Lynn Fontanne. He has produced the works of established and new playwrights in both classical and postmodern drama. In addition, for over more than forty years from 1950 to the present, Whitehead's interests and organizational skills have kept him in a broad spectrum of positions in the theatre world. He has served on the permanent panel of the U.S. State Department's Cultural Presentation Program; he has been a trustee of the American Shakespeare Theatre Festival at Stratford, Connecticut, a member of the League of New York Theatres (Past President, Board of Governors, and Secretary), the President of Neighborhood Playhouse NHC, Managing Director of ANTA, and Executive Producer and cofounder of the Producers Theatre. He has been the recipient of the Sam S. Shubert Foundation Award (1973), the Edwin Booth Award (1990), and the United Jewish Federation Lifetime Achievement Award (1991).

Withal, an occasional disappointment has plagued Whitehead during his career. One pursuit in the 1960s had a less-than-perfect outcome but did not diminish his involvement with theatre production. The hapless venture began when New York City's theatre community expressed a strong need for a permanent, national resident company comparable to one that had long been part of Britain's theatre world. At the time, Robert Whitehead (with director Elia Kazan) acted on the apparent need and formed a new repertory company to be part of a huge theatre complex then under construction, Lincoln Center for the Performing Arts. Expectations for the venture were high, with promised new plays by Arthur Miller—*After the Fall* and *Incident at Vichy*. However, from lack of financial support, Whitehead's efforts to build and maintain the company at Lincoln Center were disappointing, as were those of subsequent production teams headed by Herbert Blau and Jules Irving in 1965, by Joseph Papp in 1973, and by Richmond Crinkley in 1980. Yet Whitehead's lack of full success with the Lincoln Center project did not narrow his slot in New York City's theatre community.

A more retrospective view of Whitehead's career shows much breadth and diversity in his theatre roles. In the 1930s, Whitehead, like his cousin Hume Cronyn, entered theatre as an actor; but by the 1940s, Whitehead's involvement in production had begun with three plays (*Medea, Crime and Punishment*, and *The Member of the Wedding*), projects that soon led to his appointment as managing director for ANTA. There, in the early 1950s, he produced *Desire under the Elms* and *Golden Boy* before founding the Producers Theatre in 1953 and serving as its executive producer. At that post, the numerous plays Whitehead developed stretched into the 1960s and included *The Emperor's Clothes, Bus Stop, Much Ado about Nothing*, and *A Man for All Seasons*, the latter receiving five Antoinette Perry (Tony) Awards. (A list of his productions from the 1970s to the present appears at the end of this section.)[1]

Today, Whitehead still participates actively in annual theatre conferences as a member of symposiums. At a recent one, the Fifteenth Annual William Inge Theatre Festival, April 1996, Whitehead joined playwrights August Wilson, Robert Anderson, Jerome Lawrence, and director Josephine Abady on a panel, "The Producer, the Director, and the Playwright," to discuss the need for smooth interaction between figures who create playscripts and performance. The panel's focus on the harmony crucial to moving playscripts to audiences matched the emphasis that has been unremitting in Whitehead's career. After the symposium, the informal question-answer exchange between the director Abady and the playwrights Wilson, Lawrence, and Anderson showed their awareness of the broad canvas of American Theatre fostered by the producer Whitehead's ongoing creativity.

NOTE

1. A partial list of other productions by Robert Whitehead from the 1970s to the 1990s: *Bequest to the Nation* (1970); *The Creation of the World and Other Business*

4

The Producer's Interaction with the Theatre Team in Musical Theatre, 1940 to the Present

Many musical theatre producers have achieved star status with their audiences. From 1940 to the present, names like Richard Rodgers, David Merrick, and Harold Prince have been as well known as those of the actors starring in their musicals. Today, Harold Prince's name looms from Broadway theatre marquees for smash hits like 1996's *Kiss of the Spider Woman* (Terrence McNally). Analysis of Rodgers's, Merrick's, and Prince's rehearsal interaction with their theatre teams reveals both the stress and the success of moving their plays to the stage.

RICHARD RODGERS

Decades before Merrick's or Prince's names made headlines in musical theatre, producer-composer Richard Rodgers had begun efforts to upgrade musical theatre scores. Rodgers's views on his methods of production appear in his 1978 autobiography, *Musical Stages*. Written after decades of producing or coproducing his own and other composers' work (as well as nonmusical theatre), his comments reveal his modus operandi in moving a score to the stage.

Rodgers (1978) wrote, "On the way to an audience, [producers and playwrights] are constantly polishing and making changes; through trial and error they learn what makes dialogue funny or touching and what makes material not only suitable but remembered" (41). As Rodgers coproduced shows with "hit-maker" George Abbott in the 1940s and 1950s, and on his own in the 1960s and 1970s at the Music Theatre of Lincoln

Center, he characteristically sought scripts with innovative features, which he insisted on staging freshly. As a producer, Rodgers worked on the theory that the distinctive characteristic of theatre is "simply that it's alive" (266).

Rodgers, like many producers, spoke of a script as "frozen" after he had taken a play through out-of-town tryouts to smooth it out. The term implied that the play was in need of no more changes. However, Rodgers's production policy was that after a premiere had been "frozen," its performance could never again be "put into a can like a movie or a television program to be taken out and shown without change" (266). In addition, he cautioned that producers must keep each production fresh by requiring rehearsals to ensure that future audiences get "the best performance possible" (266). In practice, moreover, "last minute crises— anything from a torn curtain to a broken toe—must be faced and overcome" (266).

Rodgers, whose other stress in production was the need for a collaborative effort by all involved with a project, wrote that theatre is never produced "by a single person" (306). Though on one night a producer opens a successful show, "It's because one, two, three, or more people sat down and sweated over an idea that somehow clicked and broke loose" (327).

The challenges today's production teams may face when they choose an innovative project are not too different from those that confronted young Richard Rodgers early in his career as a composer, before he had begun producing musical theatre himself. In the 1940s, Rodgers and his lyricist, Larry Hart, faced dire problems with producer George Abbott on their musical score for *Pal Joey*, whose book was written by John O'Hara. Abbott was not enthusiastic about Rodgers's bent for presenting a radically new type of theatre to an audience.

In the 1930s and 1940s, musicals were generally stereotyped and exaggerated, with no literate book, little substance, and scant character development. Exceptions were magna opera like Jerome Kern's *Showboat* and George and Ira Gershwin's *Porgy and Bess*. Rodgers was sometimes baffled and temporarily blocked by producer George Abbott's lack of cooperation with him and others involved in the staging. The producer refused to be responsible for adequate salary commitments, for funding the score, for hiring sufficient actors, and for supervising the design of the score. Yet Rodgers avoided any open breaks with Abbott and persisted in his own resolve to get the play to the stage, motivated by his wish to help the promising new movement in musicals survive by stressing the interaction of song, play, and movement (Gordon Craig 1956, 252).

Rodgers's autobiography includes an account of his fortuitous involvement in that early period with the production of *Pal Joey*, notwithstanding frequent disagreements with Abbott. *Pal Joey's* score was a precursor of many that Rodgers, as producer-composer or coproducer, would handle decades later when similar concept-musicals would eventually crowd out the older, less-substantial forms. *Pal Joey*, a particularly innovative undertaking, was a dramatization of author John O'Hara's novel of the same title. Rodgers was aware that the content and style of *Pal Joey* were far ahead of its period. In his account of its preparation for the stage, Rodgers mentions repeatedly that he was attempting something new for mid-twentieth century musical comedy. His final statement registers pride in his and his partner's efforts to cooperate with producer Abbott and with author O'Hara, designer Jo Mielziner, choreographer Bob Alton, and actors Gene Kelly and Vivienne Segal as they faced and resolved squabbles on rewriting of script, design of set, and performance of music.

On the script's trip to the stage, the entire team had involved themselves in interpreting the work artistically and in staying true to the original characterization of the author's hero and heroine. They matched the music, lyrics, and design to the author's intentions and produced a mature, well-integrated work rather than one bearing the loose, poorly coordinated style of many in their decade.

DAVID MERRICK

Annals of musical production show similar stress during the career of David Merrick, whose relationships with his peer producers earned him the epithet "The Abominable Showman" (Kissel 1993, 7). In a 1993 biography of David Merrick, a critic wrote, "Some producers prefer to work quietly behind the scenes. David Merrick, practically from the beginning of his career, tended to be part of the show" (Kissel 1993, 7). Other critics have called Merrick "enigmatic and even distasteful in his methods of operation"; yet they agree that he achieved his goal of "maintaining the vitality of Broadway" (Coven, King, and Albertus 1993, xiv). *Fanny* (1954), *Hello Dolly* (1964), and *42nd Street* (1980) were among the most popular draws of their era. Critics also credit Merrick with "an essential creative gift—an ability to instill in everyone working on a given project such incalculable fear that they did the best work of which they were capable" (Coven, King, and Albertus 1993, 510). Whether such an ability can be construed as "creative" in an artistic sense is open to conjecture. Yet if "best work" implies the careful envisioning of authors' scripts by directors, designers, and actors during staging, Merrick's fear tactics could be said to foster artistic interpretation. Certainly "creative" were Merrick's imaginative merchandising stunts by which he "managed to market even some of his poorest shows, giving them a long life and profitability" (Coven, King, and Albertus 1993, xi). Notwithstanding these weak shows repeatedly made, Merrick's supporters still contend that their financial success attracted backers, "allowing him to finance more shows and stage serious plays that would not normally be financially viable on Broadway" (Coven, King, and Albertus 1993, xi). For that feat, biographer Kissel (1993) writes that Merrick's life, for all its crassness, was also "a life in the theater" (510).

Merrick's influence on musical theatre is recognized by Kissel (1993), who comments, "Musicals that, in their time, were regarded as nothing more than diversions for tired businessmen, are now studied in university theater departments" (507). A 1993 annotated bibliography, moreover, cites Merrick's sponsorship during the 1960s and 1970s of serious drama as well as musicals. "His perseverance and personal income brought many award-winning plays to Broadway—plays such as *Beckett*, *A Taste of Honey*, *Luther*, and *Marat/Sade*—which would otherwise never have been commercially staged (Coven, King, and Albertus 1993, xiii). Merrick's supporters attribute his support of serious drama to his belief that "a commercial producer also owed something to the basic art form of the stage" (Coven, King, and Albertus 1993, x). Other theatre figures of his time were less positive about Merrick's stated principles. If his supporters were correct and if he, in fact, had followed his oft-stated principles, Merrick's motivation would be laudable. His commercial success, however, did enable him to found the David Merrick Foundation "to finance serious plays he felt deserved professional production but would incur a financial risk for his loyal backers" (Coven, King, and Albertus 1993, x). Through his foundation's sponsorship, American audiences have become familiar with dramatists from abroad, among them John Osborne, Jean Anouilh, Tom Stoppard, and Peter Weiss.

HAROLD PRINCE

In the 1970s, another producer, Harold Prince, moved beyond the customary functions of production management and involved himself fully in the actual staging of scores and their books. For theatre audiences, Prince's name evokes titles produced in collaboration with Andrew Lloyd Webber—*Evita* (1978), *Fiddler on the Roof* (1964), *Phantom of the Opera* (1978), and *Cabaret* (1966, 1987)—and with Stephen Sondheim—*A Little Night Music* (1978), *Follies* (1978), and *Sweeney Todd* (1979, 1984). On Broadway in 1996, Prince's musical version of *The Kiss of the Spider Woman* (book by Terrence McNally, score by John Kander and Fred Ebb, and Prince as producer-director) adds to the list of his commercial successes.

For his early innovations in musicals, Prince is widely credited with "profoundly altering the form, style, emphasis, and tone" of musical theater (Coven, King, and Albertus 1993, xvii). Prince was an early developer of a new form of musical, one that critic Martin Gottfried, in 1972, named "the concept musical"; Gottfried (1972) declared that Prince and his theatre teams "moved Musical Theater to a new plateau" (*New York Times*, 25 April, sec. 2, 1–5). The new form fashioned all theatrical elements around a central theme, and plot figured less prominently than in standard musicals. In *Sweeney Todd*, for example, the music, lyrics, and book bolstered the spine of the play, which was "the effect of industrialization on people's souls"; in *Follies*, it was "nostalgia" (Coven, King, and Albertus 1993, xv).

Prince's productions, specifically *Cabaret*, *Sweeney Todd*, and *Evita*, brought him full media attention and established his reputation on Broadway. Of *Cabaret*, Walter Kerr of the *New York Times* wrote that the show was "stunning" (21 April 1971, sec. 2, 1–5). Richard P. Cooke, in the *Wall Street Journal*, called it "one of the most exciting, imaginative, and effective musicals to come to Broadway this year or any other" (22 November 1966, 6).

Prince moved beyond musical theatre to opera and produced *Ashmedai* for the New York City Opera Company in 1976. His production brought praise from *Opera News* critic Robert J. Jacobson (1976) for its "devastating theatricality, as devised by Prince," and for "its magically mesmerizing staging" (32). Reviewing his production of another opera, *Silverlake*, Robert J. Jacobson (1980) called Prince "a master of taste and style" (*Opera News*, 30). Of his 1981 production of *Willie Stark*, Scott Heumann (1981) said that Prince "worked his usual stage magic, employed his singers sensitively, his epic vision always in the service of the work" (*Opera News*, 30).

Tributes like these, for his innovative work in musical theatre and opera, suggest that as a producer, Harold Prince's involvement with the art of theatre transcends monetary concerns and ranges into sensitive matters of theory and practice. Understandably, Prince's artistic involvement in theatre in the last decade—*Phantom of the Opera* (1978); *Faust* (1990); *Grandchild of Kings* (1992); and his most recent production, *Kiss of the Spider Woman* (1996)—has moved him increasingly into the role of director as well as producer. His success, particularly with the many long-running productions of Terrence McNally's *Kiss of the Spider Woman*, continues to lift his star status with today's critical and popular audiences.

PART II
THE DIRECTOR

5

The Director's Role

Directors play many parts in production, depending upon the type of theatre group with which they affiliate—a commercial theatre, a repertory group, an educational theatre facility. The roles at such diverse venues will show distinct modes of interaction, authority, and responsibility. The range and the depth of directors' involvement at a venue can hinge upon the philosophy of the venue—its stance on the relevance of drama to society.

At whatever theatre facility, a director might soon protest facetiously, "When the millennium arrives, what responsibilities remain that have not already been put upon directors?" In 1905, theorist-essayist-designer Gordon Craig specified in "On the Art of the Theatre" that "the directorial function is fully established as the art of synthesizing script, design, and performance into a unique and splendid theatrical event" (quoted in Cohen 1983, 141). In 1913, Jacques Copeau added, "the director's primary task is the faithful translation of the dramatist's script into a 'poetry of the theatre' " (quoted in Brockett 1982, 578). By the 1970s, authors of theatre texts were proclaiming, "the director is the final authority in all matters related to production; he stages the play, coaches the actors, integrates the entire production" (Sievers, Stiver, and Kahan 1974, 11). In the 1980s, a popular theatre survey called the director's art "conceptualizing the play, giving it vision and purpose, inspiring and coordinating the company of artists on the theatre team" (Cohen 1983, 138).

Ironically, at many venues today, a chronic consideration in directors' conceptualizing of a play has slipped into a slot called "improving the play." Interestingly, one Shakespeare scholar has claimed, "To improve Shakespeare is more than a duty; to those who can meet the challenge it becomes a pleasure" (Bradbrook 1990, 229). The statement is less provocative if one reads the sentence that follows it: "This means, of course, not to surpass him but to improve the occasion, to bring him forward, project him into the present" (Bradbrook 1990, 229). Thus the constant concern of directors is less for the play's past than for its vibrancy in the present and its place in the future.

To give the play life and endurance takes a creative bent and painstaking planning. Directors develop their blueprint for decor, costuming, and style of presentation early so that a scale model can be prepared and sufficient time allowed for construction of backdrops, sets, and props. If the director's intentions for the scripted sets show him ignoring practicality while the producer pushes economy, a compromise must ensue. Fairly early, too, the director must compose stage pictures, arrange groupings, give scenes visual patterns. He may find these in the script or in the subtext or in his own imagination. Unlike decisions on decor, the planning of stage pictures can take place gradually, inspired by the director's opportunity to watch the actors at rehearsal sessions.

For both classic and modern plays, seasoned directors can discern what is at the heart of a scene, how best to stage this center whether it is an external character clash or an inner emotional conflict. Though the script itself may indicate to actors where the most dynamic points lie, the director can illustrate techniques to help actors "build a scene or a speech in a climactic manner" (Schneider 1986, 198). The director might suggest body language or stage behavior to add force to the scene (Cohen 1983, 89).

Directors may also help actors broaden the gamut of emotions requisite for effective stage voices. Intuitive directors will consider whether to suggest to an actor specific vocal tones, levels, rate of speaking—or whether to refrain from comment and let the actor judge his work for himself (Schneider 1986, 143). In these instances, the seasoned director "can gradually FREE the performers to experience their own imagination and sensitivity" (Schneider 1986, 143).

Some directors excel at helping actors with character motivation. Still, producer and sometime actor-director George Abbott once remarked that he wanted "none of that motivation business to confuse him," and needed only hints for moves and blocking (Schneider 1986, 212). Yet at times directors may need to help actors find what drives their characters; in even more instances, the director may need to help actors project that motivating impulse to the audience.

A creative opportunity for many directors arises when they have a part in orchestrating the component of sound in production—for example, telephone, footsteps, shrieks, sighs, offstage rumbles. Directors sometimes add sounds to connect awkward spots in the staging. In one production of Beckett's *Ohio Impromptu*, a director added the sound of sharp knocks on the wooden table at which Listener and Reader sit; the bony knocks nicely linked the many moments when Beckett's script calls for seconds of total darkness. At times, directors have supplemented the scripted sound for Tennessee Williams's *The Glass Menagerie*, adding a second waltz to the Gentleman Caller's scene in the living room with Laura.

Opportunity for directorial choice also surfaces when questions arise on what should loom on stage in the play's last moments. The self-interest of an actor may challenge a director's vision of what or who gets the final spotlight. Is the choice one the director can intuit from the text and/or subtext? Perhaps repeated rehearsal or rereadings of the text will provide the answer.

Developing a Shakespearean play for performance can often present a dilemma for directors whose theatres attract audiences of dissimilar taste and background. Some viewers prefer thoughtful, conventional stagings of Shakespeare's classics; others want up-to-date, sparkling versions of his texts. If theatre groups set out to attract new and untrained theatre audiences, should they try to sell modern, captivating revisions of Shakespeare or sidestep what traditional viewers may consider profanations of his language and poetry? Some producers may ask themselves, "Why can't a production be both colorful and thoughtful, slick and provocative, and in every way an explication of the text, visually and aurally?" (Loney 1990, xiv).

Through such staging care and decisions, directors determine the ultimate imprint the play leaves on its audiences. At curtain, the performance will have shown the playscript's intent—to agitate, to amuse, to alert, to pacify, or to alienate the audience.

6

Interviews, Personal Accounts, Comments by Directors

To grasp the complexity of directors' functioning, one has only to read closely the personal accounts, comments in seminars, or other exegeses by directors—whether new or tried-and-tested, from various theatre venues. Their goals, production philosophies, and interrelationships with their theatre teams become clear to us. Their expectations, guidelines, and techniques permeate their accounts; in all, they appear to follow lines of authority and responsibility in moving great theatre to their audiences.

In excerpts from directors' published overviews of theatre, from their interviews with critics, and from seminars in which they expound upon their production problems and successes, we comprehend their directorial principles and operational methods as they take us inside theatre's production ring from the 1970s to the present.

Director David Sievers: Excerpt from "Realization of the Scope of the Theatrical Production," in *Directing for the Theatre*

The neophyte director should not stand in awe or fear at the number of tasks that need to be performed for a smoothly-running production. In many cases he will find help from unexpected sources if he will but seek it. The important thing is that before and during his preparation as a

he needs to be completely and constantly aware of the scope of
production elements.

irector is responsible for staging the play, coaching the actors
and integrating the entire production. In order to achieve a unified impression upon the audience, the director must be the final authority in
all matters related to the production. Too many cooks have spoiled more
than one theatrical broth.

The foregoing statement does not, however, preclude the director's
using his authority sparingly and applying the best psychological principles of leadership, which include welcoming and encouraging creative
contributions from others, consulting with his staff before making decisions, explaining his reasons rather than being arbitrary, respecting the
special talents and training of his staff, and giving the entire team a sense
of participation in the creative process. (11–12)

Director Alan Schneider: Excerpt from "What's Prologue Is Past," *Entrances*

For most of my working life, I have managed to earn my living at what
I have liked doing the most: directing plays on the stage with actors.
Whether this happened to be in the New York theater or elsewhere did
not affect my attitude or manner for working. I've directed plays on
almost every size and shape of stage, from those with a proscenium, now
almost a historic form, to theater-in-the-round, the use of which I helped
to pioneer, as well as three-quarters round, thrust stage, and almost
everything else in between. I have held rehearsals in attics, lofts, store-
rooms, washrooms, boiler factories, gymnasiums, churches—and occa-
sionally, even in theaters. I have put on plays in tiny auditoriums where
the actors tripped over the first rows of spectators and in amphitheaters
that would have been too vast for [Max] Reinhardt. I have worked in-
doors and out, on classics and inexperienced first drafts—the best and
the worst—and the only virtue in all this is that I kept on working.

Always I have persisted, regardless of reception or results. Which is
what Samuel Beckett in particular has taught me, through his plays and
the example of his life. In spite of everything, one goes on, with or without sand in the bags. In the theater, as well as in all artistic endeavors,
the only thing that counts is the work itself and the need to go on with
it to the highest possible level, with the most personal concentration. It
was Beckett who taught me not to be distracted or disturbed by success
or failure, by praise or blame, by surface or show, analysis or distraction,
self-criticism or the criticism of others. (xiii–xv)

Directors Michael Kahn and Frank Dunlop and Producers- Directors Bernard Gersten and Harvey Lichtenstein

Assembled comments and perspectives from City University of New York (C.U.N.Y.) Seminar, "Problems in Staging Shakespeare" (edited by Dr. Glenn Loney, Professor Emeritus at the City University of New York, in *Staging Shakespeare*, 1990).

Michael Kahn: [A huge theatre] is not conducive to creating any kind of real actor-audience relationship. It also runs into another problem because it is so large: The actor has to have certain skills in order to make his points in that theatre. It's very comforting for an actor to work in the [tiny] Mitzi Newhouse theatre [Lincoln Center, New York City]. . . . Over the years in America, the training has been towards a kind of greater intimacy of portrayal and the importance of small moments. . . . It has been increasingly difficult to find actors who can make their points, who can create characters, who can fulfill moments in a theatre as large and unfocused as the American Shakespeare Theatre [New York City]. It's healthy to try, though, because one of the things I would hate to see us get away from is the largeness of Shakespeare.

Bernard Gersten: [If] you are choosing to play to an audience that has never been to the theatre, does that obviously influence the way in which you do a play?

Frank Dunlop: No.

Bernard Gersten: We're not talking about how you organize the auditorium. But once they're in there, if you are trying to attract an audience who's never seen a play before, do you find yourself having to stage-produce a play in a special way for them?

Frank Dunlop: No. I've [directed] a play for the Royal Shakespeare, *Sherlock Holmes*, by William Gillette (subsequently imported for Broadway and an American tour). . . . I did it exactly the same as I do any play. If I'm [directing] a play for a commercial management that's meant to make a hell of a lot of money, and the people are going to pay whatever they pay on the front row in New York or London, I still have the same attitude. I do everything as though I'm seeing it, thinking about it, for the first time. If I'm doing *Twelfth Night* for the twentieth time, I don't think, "Oh, that audience has seen it before and so on." I still must do it as though it is being done for the first time.

Michael Kahn: Coming over here today, I thought that's what I'd say about how I work. One has supposedly done this kind of production, and one has done an anti-war production, and one has done a pop production, or a rock production, and you think, "No, I've really just done a play." I've just simply read the text, as I do all the time, over and over again as though it's a new play. I keep trying to tell myself this is by Neil Simon or somebody, and it's never been done before; it doesn't have a history; it isn't in the cultural pantheon; it's just a new play. You want to approach it as a new play, and you want the audience to see it as if it's a new play.

Harvey Lichtenstein: How do you cope with the size of the Opera House stage at the Brooklyn Academy of Music?

Frank Dunlop: Well, we build another stage. After working at the Young Vic, which is very like the Shakespearean theatre, we were going to work some of the festivals. The first year around Europe, we were having to go to opera houses. . . . We realized that we could actually get in the middle of the audience by building the stage out, playing out across the front of the stage, and getting a lot of the audience up on the stage behind us, so that we've got audience on two sides. Now, that's much more difficult than having audience on three sides, because they're two separate blocks. But they presented a very different challenge from the normal operatic theatre convention, and it broke the audience's preconceived attitudes to watching a play. We stopped doing that. We think that we ought not to perform in proscenium theatres at all.

Michael Kahn: I've tried every way to fight that problem. Frank is right, and, as I said earlier, I think the theatre at Stratford is really a liability in terms of reaching the audience, in that there is a separation. Why don't I change that? As you know, over the years the stage has moved, crept out into the audience, and now it's a bastard thrust. The best solution would be just to take it apart and put it all in the middle. What I try to do is to reduce the size of the stage in every possible way so that one does not have to do a spectacle to fill it up. That means making a smaller playing area. If there's been any style of production, it's been taking place somewhere in the middle and down front of the proscenium on a smaller stage built on the big one.

I think one of the things an actor has to do, in order to get away from an "operatic" performance in a theatre that seats fifteen hundred people, is to give the kind of physical performance that communicates much with the body rather than just having to "emote largely."

Harvey Lichtenstein: What about dress and decor? Do you have any ideas, any style, any feeling about productions in a certain dress or decor?

Michael Kahn: Stratford was certainly the most at fault in this area at one time. One felt, when watching a production, that one wasn't seeing the play—one was seeing Goya or Velásquez or Manet. I think that replaced a real engagement with the play. It replaced an idea about the play with a decor idea. I would try to limit it at the time to three choices: One would be to do the play in the period in which it was written— Elizabethan or Jacobean. Or, to do it in the period it was written about, or to do it in modern dress—since the plays were obviously modern-dress productions when they were done in Shakespeare's time.

I still react against productions when I feel the choice of setting and decor inhibits the meaning of the play. . . . Even saying, "Well, this is an anti-war play," begins to make Shakespeare less interesting than he is. What is interesting about Shakespeare is that you cannot categorize him that easily. Choosing a period like eighteenth-century Napoleonic, for instance, either reminds you of something else or makes the play less rich. To turn *Way of the World* into Oscar Wilde is a mistake. It seems to make *Way of the World* less interesting and makes you want to see *The Importance of Being Earnest*.

Frank Dunlop: I've done terrible, extreme things when I was at the National [England], because there was a lot of money, and you tend to put on more and more scenery to entertain the audience with what you do with the back wall of that stage. It's something I don't think you can avoid in the sort of theatre one is often presented with. It's appalling that one has to spend so much time, energy, and money. This different, bloody, titillating construction has nothing to do with what goes on between the actor and the audience. . . .

Michael Kahn: I find settings terribly important. I hate the fact that one has to do them in advance of rehearsal, that one can't make them up around the third week of rehearsal; that's about when one has some idea about what is needed and what one would like. . . . It's a repertory theatre, and everything has to be done a month or two in advance. I suspect that what I try to look for is something that does not say what the play is about. I don't think that the set should make the statement but should somehow create as neutral an atmosphere as possible.

Frank Dunlop: You are having to make a statement behind the actors.

Michael Kahn: To occupy the space, at any rate.

Frank Dunlop: Once you occupy the space, you must think exactly what you are going to say there [and send it in] to be made before the first day's work with the actors. This is utter nonsense. You don't know what marvelous things are going to come out of twenty people working together and creating.

Michael Kahn: At Stratford, Ontario, although the answer seems architectural, it is still a statement. Although it is a playing area, you finally do everything against brown wood with the same doors. At Juilliard, I have a set that I do everything on, and it's really rather like that. It's infinitely easier, and it makes the rhythm of the plays interesting, but even that is a kind of statement.

Frank Dunlop: At Stratford, the statement that's made up on that stage architecturally is an Elizabethan statement. I think it's quite difficult now . . . but if you get a really good architect, he can create a place where you can work.

Moderator: "Can modern dress add anything meaningful to a production?"

Michael Kahn: It's an extraordinary thing. I [directed] a production of *Love's Labour's Lost*. It was the first modern-dress production I'd ever done, and *Love's Labour's Lost* is a reasonably complicated text for audiences to understand. Literally, because I set it that way, the audience understood everything. I got a lot of letters [objecting], "How dare you rewrite the text?" I had not rewritten anything. I had added a few lines, because I had decided on modern dress. I thought it was fair game, since the play was a satire on the Earl of Southampton's circle. These were obviously recognizable personages in Shakespeare's time. I felt it was perfectly okay for me to substitute recognizable personages of our own time; so it was filled with the Beatles and Truman Capote and Lee Radziwill and Mia Farrow. At least I knew that's who they were.

Bernard Gersten: But you substituted common personages for royal personages.

Michael Kahn: No, no. Lee Radziwill, Mia Farrow, and those people are the royalty of our time. The audience absolutely understood everything. They laughed at Elizabethan puns; it was quite extraordinary. The year before, I had done a production that I thought was extremely together—*Merchant of Venice*. I thought it was about money and commerce, and I set it in the Renaissance. Everybody thought it was really rather dear. A lot of people came only because it was Renaissance clothes, [but they] didn't listen. . . . [The] people who did listen understood. In an odd way, to get people really to listen to Shakespeare, you have to break their expectations. Sometimes one goes overboard doing it; sometimes one finds the right way.

Bernard Gersten: I remember when I entered the Billy Rose Theatre to see [Peter] Brook's [A] *Midsummer Night's Dream*, the white light was really blasting onto the stage from the moment the audience came in. And the audience was sitting there in the reflected light, literally bathed in it. Exactly what Michael [Kahn] referred to was taking place during the fifteen minutes I was there before the play began. Everybody was sitting forward, and there must have been doubts from certain people stunned by the light. One of the things that struck me most sharply about the RSC's *Richard II* was that the whole stage was bathed in gray. . . . It depressed me and cast me down. But I sat at that *Dream* and half-watched the play and half-watched the people. They were listening to the lines that so often lull audiences to sleep, lines they knew they could count on—the measured treads. They listened and they heard. The entire reaction to that production was fresh.

Michael Kahn: I started out by thinking that you must make Shakespeare "relevant." That word violently upsets me now. I tried to find ways to make Shakespeare speak in production terms—to have people swinging from the ceiling, loud music.

Frank Dunlop: And be one-legged.

Michael Kahn: Yes, one-legged, with a lot of peeing on the floor. Now I've come to think that sort of thing pigeonholes Shakespeare and makes it smaller and less "relevant" because it replaces Shakespeare's mind with substitutes.

Moderator: "What good is it to do a museum piece, if you have nobody coming?"

Michael Kahn: You must be very careful. A museum piece has very little to do with decor. I think there's a lot of fuss about the fact that if you set a play in the Renaissance because it deals with that period, then immediately it's old. One of the most modern productions of *Romeo and Juliet* I ever saw was Franco Zeffirelli's stage production, set in the Renaissance. It was absolutely contemporary and alive—at least until the last act! It was done absolutely period, but it had to do with a relationship of the director and actors to the text and to the life they created.

Bernard Gersten: Of course, but that's always been true.

Michael Kahn: Classical theatre must not be a museum. It must be investigation.

Moderator: I think a lot of that has to do with making choices. I saw the [Tyrone] Guthrie production of *The Merchant of Venice*. It was highly traditional and a very good production. It had nothing to do with making it current or updating it. It was just very good acting and good directing.

Bernard Gersten: There's no substitute. It doesn't matter what clothes you put on, or what clothes you fail to put on. There are no substitutes for the talent of the actors and the skill of the director—then, into the text.

Michael Kahn: That's the answer.

Bernard Gersten: You can always buy costumes without limit—depending upon how much money you have—and decor from now until doomsday. But these are not substitutes. The virtue of our production of *Much Ado* was the relationship between Beatrice and Benedict that transcended any antic behavior of the Keystone Cops in the show. Sam Waterston as Benedict realized that part to a greater extent than any of a half dozen Benedicts I've known and variously liked. He could have worn anything. The couple could have done it in their rehearsal clothes on this platform, and it wouldn't have mattered.

Moderator: Let's not put traditional theatre into one category, and, in another category, put modern, wild, avant-garde production.

Bernard Gersten: It's too neat and packaged. I don't think the reality of preparing plays responds to that kind of packaging. Nobody sets out to say, "I will now do a traditional production!" How would you define it? What defines the costumes as traditional in the [Tyrone] Guthrie production of *Merchant*? What fulfilled that production was not that the costumes were traditional; it was the fullness of the play.

Frank Dunlop: My first duty is to see that the play is absolutely clear—to get over what the words mean, what the situations and characters are. The means I would like to rule out are those which are done for different effects in order to express one's self as an artist.

Moderator: But then you walk into [Peter] Brook's *Dream* and see some amazing effects.

Michael Kahn: I saw it in Stratford in the middle of a very dreary season. Suddenly out came the *Dream*. After one got over the white box, one finally realized it was just a rehearsal studio, and that all kinds of marvelous, tricky things were rehearsal props in Day-Glo colors. What was astonishing about the production was its clarity, as opposed to other productions where we've seen people throw themselves around and jump from the ceiling. The text was clear; I heard things in the production that I had never heard in that play before.

Frank Dunlop: I think the reason they do those shock things at the beginning is to jolt people sitting there with a conventional attitude. Unless you jolt them, they just sit there. At the Old Vic, *Love's Labour's Lost* was a great example. I was going to codirect it, and half way through the first day's rehearsal, I suddenly realized what it was going to be. I went to Larry Olivier and said, "Look, I cannot do this with you because I know what you [would] force me to do in this production." When it came to opening night, there was exquisitely lit decor, all pinks and blues and greens. From the first word, you knew it was going to be beautifully spoken in the English tradition. The whole audience [murmured] "AAAAAAHHHHHH." It was like lying in warm, shallow water, and it was a great experience for them for about—it seemed like ten hours. Most of those people were asleep in the second act, because it was respectful to Shakespeare. The whole operation—you couldn't knock it down.

Moderator: I saw Mr. Kahn's modern version of *Love's Labour's Lost* at Stratford a few years ago. We saw motorcycles come out and young people with masses of curly hair. . . . By the end of the play, we said, "Well, this is interesting, and now we're part of the scene." But it wasn't what we remembered of Shakespeare. In New York, when they did [Peter] Brook's [A] *Midsummer Night's Dream*, I went with my three married children and their mates. They loved everything. I kept seeing it as a beautiful circus spectacle, acrobatics here, there, and everywhere.

Bernard Gersten: I must tell you this—I didn't see Michael's production of *Love's Labour's Lost*, but from your description, I'm so sorry to have missed it. You must understand that everybody who does a Shakespearean play today, unless he has done them repeatedly in conventional fashion, investigates the play every time as [if] for the first time. I'm sure every time Frank does *The Taming of the Shrew*, he approaches it in a fresh way. . . . You should be as open as you can. What's wrong with a circus? Circuses are fine in the theatre. The day I saw that *Dream*, people—young, middle, and old—were listening to the words and to what was happening to believable, creditable people on stage. The fact that they did some circus tricks incidentally didn't matter a bit.

Michael Kahn: I never think I'm going to do an avant-garde production or a traditional production. The year that you saw *Love's Labour's Lost*, I also did a very traditional (in your terms) production of *Richard II*. I'm very eclectic. . . . A play strikes me at a given time in a given way.

(N.B.: In the decades before 1990, Michael Kahn was Producing Director of the McCarter Theatre at Princeton University and is currently at Folger Theatre in Washington, D.C. Frank Dunlop, former director for London's Young Vic, staged *[The] Taming of the Shrew* and *Scapino* for American audiences. Bernard Gersten was formerly Associate Producer of New York's Shakespeare Festival. Harvey Lichtenstein was a producer at the Brooklyn Academy.)

Director Sidney Berger

Excerpts from an interview with Sidney Berger, Director of the University of Houston's School of Theatre, 1994.

Question: Is the director's goal, his overall task, about the same whether he is in a professional, regional, or academic venue?

Dr. Berger: When you're the director, the task is the realization through you—through you and the actors—of the material of the play; and you have to bring that creation and living solution onto the stage. A director to my mind is not a "stage-er," not someone who makes pictures; a director is someone who takes the print off the page and helps translate it into living terms. The director is the controlling element, the one who has to guide the production. There is one governing eye; that in my mind has got to be the director. Sometimes the playwright gets mistreated because the director is too self-absorbed or is very heavy-handed. There are a thousand reasons. For example, Alan Schneider did such a great job with Edward Albee's plays in the sixties because he was a brilliant director and the match of a brilliant playwright.

Question: Are playwrights often in attendance at rehearsals?

Dr. Berger: If I do a [David] Mamet or a [Sam] Shepard play here at the university, they're simply not going to appear at rehearsals. When I did Harold Pinter's *Betrayal* last year at a professional theatre in the city, I felt my job in producing that play in the absence of the author was to be as scrupulously honest to what that playwright wrote as I could be, given the circumstances I was in. Pinter was not there to say, "Well, I don't like the space that you are working in" or "I don't like that actor."

Question: Can you give a more specific example of that phrase you mentioned before—your phrase "given the circumstances"?

Dr. Berger: Yes. You've got to remember that when a director sets to work, he has a very specific set of circumstances. (Don't mind me for using "he" interchangeably—it's a generic word.) The actors' personalities are radically different no matter where the director works. The space I work in, the budget of that theatre, the philosophy of that theatre, the producer, all of that has to do with the nature of my production. When I go to the Alley and direct a play, it's another set of circumstances— even the audience complexion changes. But I don't, I can't, direct for the audience.

Question: You can't?

Dr. Berger: I can't, I don't, direct for them, because they are total strangers to me. I adjust to them. . . . But I cannot in a rehearsal for six weeks create an audience that is going to be my partner. As the great [Tyrone] Guthrie put it—I am the audience of one. I can work with the play, and I can work with the actors as my collaborators and partners. Ultimately the audience comes into the theatre, and then they become my collaborators. Because when they are there and reacting to that play, I have got to alter my work depending on what I sense from that, and they become the last stage.

Question: And then you might alter your staging?

Dr. Berger: Not "might"—I do. Let me make something clear: When I say "alter," I don't mean "pander"—I mean I can hopefully sense from an audience in previews whether something is not clear, is not clear enough, is obscure, whether the actor is missing moments and the audience is reacting and telling him—or me—that. I have to take into account all of these things. But the difference is that I don't have a whole lot of time to do that in most normal academic runs. Most university productions run five or six performances. Now when I'm directing at the Alley, it's different; and it's interesting, because I go back a lot when I have a long run. I remember when I was working with Theatre under the Stars—the producer's a good friend—and he said "Why do you keep coming back? You're not getting paid for it!" And I said, "Because I can make it better"—meaning that as I'm watching the audience, as I'm watching the actors, I can make adjustments.

Question: At previews and early performances at regional and academic venues, I often see directors standing at the back of the theatre, watching the audience.

Dr. Berger: That's telling you something, and to ignore that is foolhardy. But there's a thin line between hearing what they're telling you and pandering to an audience and therefore to yourself by saying, "If they're restless right here, I've got to do a stage trick!"—even if the director does that unconsciously. In professional theatre, directors must listen to audiences and adjust problematic spots in the staging. I'll never forget what Michael Bennett, the great choreographer/director once said to me. We were at a meeting, and he said that in *Follies*—he directed *Follies* on Broadway—there was this wonderful thing of chorus girls floating from stage right to left, or left to right, and he said "The only reason I did that was because I knew the eye would follow a moving object, and when I had a problem down left that I could not solve, I floated a girl stage right so that the eye would move away from the problem and watch that!" Now that's a trick! Well, for Bennett it was an act of desperation, but nevertheless it was a directorial deception. But when you, the director, "hear" the audience, hopefully you can solve the problem! And to do it, you try to adjust whatever is going on, on stage, to the fact that the audience is telling you "This moment is not working." That's a directorial and actor "difficulty" in the process of solution.

Question: What if a director at a university school of theatre wanted to present a play of Shakespeare's; could his students carry it off?

Dr. Berger: You're asking a very complicated question! Let's say I'm a director doing Shakespeare here at U. of H., and for another production, I'm doing Shakespeare in the park, professionally. When I do it in the park, I have very high expectations because I have a much larger pool of trained professional talent to draw from. So that when I do Shakespeare there, I can work far more with the poetry because I've got people who are trained—hopefully—and experienced in its use. But when I decide to do Shakespeare here, I should realize at the outset that I am going to deal with students who are of varying ability and experience. That's what a university is—that's what any school is. And in that case I must teach as I direct.

Question: But they're good actors.

Dr. Berger: Of course. They may be wonderful actors, but they vary in experience; they vary in training. Well, I have two chores then: Alan Schneider once said when he was at San Diego that he did not want to be a teacher while he was directing. Okay? My role when I'm directing here at U. of H. *is* to be a teacher while I'm directing. My responsibility when I'm directing at the Alley or at any professional theatre is *not* to be a teacher. When you're in an academic or conservatory environment, you are constantly teaching *as* you're directing. Now that does not mean that you are less a director than you are a teacher. It means that you have two jobs you are doing, and that you have to do both equally well. If I have young men or women who are not handling the verse competently because they have not been trained well enough, I can't go out to the audience and say, "Excuse me, Ladies and Gentlemen, but Actors L and V are just not very well trained yet, so please be nice to them." If I expect people to pay $1 or $50 to come into the theater to see the play, they deserve to see the play as well performed as possible. My job is to teach those actors in the rehearsal period as much as I can humanly teach them, and to direct the play as well as I can humanly direct it. Or else not do Shakespeare at all!

Question: Not at all?

Dr. Berger: Well, I don't do *King Lear* here; I do [A] *Comedy of Errors*, or [A] *Midsummer Night's Dream*; I do those plays I think the actors are capable of within their limitations. Sometimes those limitations can be extended—you never know what's going to happen. I saw [a student-actor], for example, in [A] *Comedy of Errors* do a superb job in that play: I never expected her to reach such heights, but she did. She's very talented but had a limited amount of training. So we did a lot of heavy teaching during that period of time, and it paid off, because ultimately she ended up with a performance of astounding quality.

My point, though, is that it is not going to be the same process that I might go through in a professional venue; but at the same time it's got to be good enough in expectation that an audience can SEE the play and still see the PLAY.

Question: You would not cut or adjust the amount of poetry in its script?

Dr. Berger: I might in Shakespeare for purposes of eliminating or substituting for archaic language, or, in extreme circumstances, because of an actor's inability. I do cut because sixteenth-century audiences were different from those in our time, and there are other exigencies as well. The canon is not to be worshipped but realistically and creatively produced. When Franco Zeffirelli did *Romeo and Juliet* (the film), he cut the potion scene: There is no potion scene in that film. And at a meeting with him, I heard a scholar take him to task for having done that; and he listened very carefully, and then in his own sweet voice he said, "Lady, I cut it because she couldn't do it."

Question: A choice instance there of directorial modification?

Dr. Berger: Of course! For if an actor cannot handle something because he/she is unable to for whatever the reasons, the director has some choices he must make with the author's script: With a play in public domain he can cut; the better option is to work with the actor until he becomes convincing; those are the choices we have to make every day in rehearsal. What is at risk, however, particularly in cutting, is the play itself. I'm very wary of simply saying "Let's cut that scene because she can't do it." Zeffirelli had a fourteen-year-old Olivia Hussey do Juliet— a fourteen-year-old in Shakespeare's time was radically different from a fourteen-year-old in our time—and he knew that he was buying one thing and was going to have to give up another. When I'm doing a Shakespeare here, as I said earlier, I'm not going to do a play that I know the students simply are incapable of handling at their level of experience and training. Now there is a theory, academically, that has been thrown at me a number of times, and that is, "You should do *King Lear*! They are students and they should know what it is like to play it." My answer is that I'm training students to perform before an audience. They are being trained to be actors or directors or designers. I'm not going to train them to be unable to function in a professional world because what I was doing was totally unreal. I'm totally opposed to that way of teaching. I will not do things that are so totally out of students' abilities that they end up failing and thinking, "Oh, failure is good for me." Failure is good for them in terms of extending their reach, not by denying them any reach at all.

Question: In professional theatre, isn't staging a script of an already-lauded play hard for a director to envision freshly and freely?

Dr. Berger: No, it's not. If I were doing a well-known play—let's take *The Glass Menagerie* again—what I find happens to me when I direct it is this: Once I walk through the rehearsal hall and the door closes, I am in a completely different world, and that world emanates to a degree from me. Everything I am, everything I have experienced, the manner in which I've grown—all affect how I start developing the play with the actors. One thing, I might add, happens from the actors' perspective: I can't do Eddie Dowling's production because I'm not Eddie Dowling; so when I start, all those models just vanish—they go away because there is no way I can put myself into those bodies.

Question: Or would even want to! When [Laurence] Olivier decided to stage Williams's much-produced *A Streetcar Named Desire*, he said he did not want to "warm up somebody else's cake"!

Dr. Berger: He was correct! He had to do the play from his own perspective! Now, that may be good, bad, indifferent, or shallow or deep; but finally, it is a singular production that evolves from the talents and personalities rehearsing it.

Question: And your phrase "from his own perspective"—the director's—he keeps his own perspective without distorting the author's intention.

Dr. Berger: Yes. He should. But in the case I cited previously from *The Glass Menagerie*, if the director doesn't have the actress blow out the candles, then he is quite consciously distorting the author's play! Let's use a classic as an example. When [Laurence] Olivier directed a *Richard II* or a *Hamlet*, it was *his* production. That is *his* view of that play: It comes from *who he is*. It is not distortion, since there is a basic loyalty to the text.

Question: Can you give me an example of what comes from the director's perspective—from "who he is"—and therefore is not directorial playwriting!!

Dr. Berger: All right. Yes. Let me give you a better example. The ghost of Hamlet's father appears. Invariably the ghost of Hamlet's father appears, invariably done with great lighting effects and clouds of fog and smoke. It never worked for me, and I didn't understand why! I did *Hamlet* several times, and that scene was never successful. The last time I did it, I stopped and thought to myself, "Why is it not working; why has it never worked for me, whether Olivier or anyone else did it successfully?" And then I remembered a friend of mine in L.A., whose mother was living with her at the time. She told me of an incident—her mother, widowed, was in the bathroom, and she saw what seemed to be the ghost of her dead husband standing in the doorway; and she said she was terrified because it was so absolutely simple and real! He was as real to her as—as you are sitting on that sofa. And it was as if you were dead but you're just sitting the way you are. She said for weeks she couldn't sleep because of that! And for whatever the reason, that came back to my memory and I thought, "Well of course, that is the whole answer. The whole answer is related to the way Shakespeare must have done it originally—which was that the father's figure was seen in full daylight at three in the afternoon: There were no smoky effects or strange strobe lights or anything else. And so when I did it, when it happened with just an actor walking out on stage with no effects at all, everyone knew that the old king was *dead*, and it became an extraordinary and very frightening moment. But, I had to discover that: It came out of an experience that I had, and out of my understanding of the play and of Shakespeare's own time; it came out of a lot of things that melded together and produced that way of doing that moment. Other directors have done that moment differently.

Question: From their own perspective—and it isn't reauthoring the play?

Dr. Berger: I'd not changed one word.

Question: Well, you're off the hook! That was a fantastic example.

Dr. Berger: It is the one that stays in my memory longest.

Director Kimber Cox

Excerpts from Interview with Kimber Cox, Graduate-Student Director at the University of Houston's School of Theatre, 1996

Question: Will you describe the type of experiences you have had in theatre up to the present?

Kimber Cox: Most of my directing experience has consisted of either student productions, church musicals, or children's theatre. This also means I have worked more extensively with student or amateur performers than with professionals.

Question: With what does the director begin the process of producing a new play?

Kimber Cox: In some cases (church musicals), I have been presented with scripts and asked to direct them and was even presented with an already chosen cast. For student productions, I chose the play and had to present a proposal to the faculty. In both instances it was my sole responsibility to decide what approach I would take to the plays. However, for the Albee Workshop, I worked very closely with the playwright and, never having [had] that opportunity before, tried extremely hard to accommodate the playwright. I must say I learned from this experience that the next time I have the opportunity to work with a playwright present, I will probably, at times, take a much stronger stand on what I consider to be script problems (if the work has never before been produced) and also make better use of the opportunity of having the playwright there to discover more about the play and his intentions.

For myself, I am usually affected by all theatre I see, but I don't believe I would be doing my job if all I did was try to duplicate a previous staging. A director would have a different cast, a different space, a different production staff, so not only would it be impossible to copy a previous staging, it would be, in my opinion, counterproductive to the purpose of theatre. This could be done by a good stage manager, and the director would be functionless.

Question: Who or what determines the possible style of production?

Kimber Cox: Theatre is, however, at its best a collaborative effort. To me, any director who did not take advantage of his designers and staff in discovering the play and its possibilities risks the likelihood of missing out on the full potential of the play. The possibilities are infinite, but with an already established production, I feel the director should avoid doing things just because this is the way it has always been done. However, he should also beware of trying things just to prove that he is innovative. Ultimately the script must support all decisions made, and they should be consistent with the overall production.

Question: Who or what determines a script's performance tempo?

Kimber Cox: It is impossible to ultimately decide who is responsible for the play's tempo. Initially it is the script itself which begins the process, but the director's choices, the demands of set and costume choices, the actors' decisions (and variations which must naturally occur with live performances), and eventually even the audience (their mood, their responses, etc.) all play an entwined part in tempo. At best these work together and are responsive to each other in creating the whole. At worst, the director and actor can sometimes unnaturally try to impose a forced tempo on a production, creating a stilted, uneven performance.

Question: How much can the director amplify or modify the author's stage directions for setting, lighting, costumes, properties, characters' delivery of lines, and movement?

Kimber Cox: To begin with, a director must determine which directions are actually the playwright's and which are the stage manager's notes from the initial production. I feel the director has some freedom in modifying directions. If he does not have the facilities and equipment to do what is asked, he must choose how best to achieve the effect that is wanted. It is important to be consistent with the overall production, and his decisions must be text supported, but it is probably better to change directions if they cannot be done effectively and well.

Question: Does the director need a scale model of the set before rehearsals begin? before blocking?

Kimber Cox: I have never had the opportunity of having a scale model to work with. Although I can see a benefit if one were available, especially if one is talking about a multilevel set, this does bring up the importance of a director having the knowledge of how to read floor plans. Scale models are a luxury, and in my experience they are often done after the fact (or during) and often not available during rehearsals.

Question: How much can directors alter the script's prescribed sound?

Kimber Cox: Sound is as important (though often overlooked) as any of the other elements of production. Anything which is consistent with the world of the play should be considered. I do believe, though, that what is done should have as much attention paid to it as everything else. If you do not have adequate equipment to do what you want, badly done sound can quickly and easily remove the audience from the world of the play.

Question: Given a choice of stages for a new play, how would the director determine the type to use—traditional, arena, thrust?

Kimber Cox: Aesthetics, economics, and availability all influence the choice of facilities, but previous staging should not be a major factor. The most important factor, however, must be the script itself and the requirements it makes. Physical farces such as *Noises Off*, which require[s] two stories and many doors, are not really practical in arena or thrust, for example. However, in more cases than not, the director's and designers' imaginations are the most important factors.

Question: What role does the director play in selecting the cast?

Kimber Cox: In some cases the producer delivers casting choices (major stars as drawing cards). If the playwright is a participant, he/she will usually have definite opinions as to who should or should not be cast.

It should be remembered, however, that the director is the one who will be working the most closely with the actors. In additions, his/her experience may often lead to the workable choice, as there is much more involved than merely the "right" look.

7

The Director's Interaction with the Theatre Team

DIRECTOR LAWRENCE SACHAROW AND THE STAGING OF EDWARD ALBEE'S *THREE TALL WOMEN*

In 1991, playwright Edward Albee directed *Three Tall Women* alone for its premiere at Vienna's English Theatre, then worked with another director, Lawrence Sacharow, for subsequent stagings in New York. The text's esoteric subject matter and style profited from the objectivity of its author and director team as they staged Albee's vision of a woman's grave engagement with maturity and maternity.

In the relationship of director Sacharow and playwright Albee during the New York production, each of the two had creative input in the formidable staging of the complex script. Albee did not act as a kind of *éminence grise* during the staging, nor did Sacharow serve as a draftsman as opposed to a collaborator.

Three Tall Women's script, like other transformational drama rooted in "America's Theatrical Renaissance," sets virtual reality against surrealistic fantasy.[1] The use of mystical characters intermingled in spirit or body with more usual beings has long been one of this playwright's enthusiasms.[2] In *Three Tall Women*, the actresses appear on stage together to portray one character—the play's composite mother-figure—at ages twenty-six, fifty-four, and ninety-two. Prior to the actresses' appearance as the three components of the mother figure, the audience will have seen one of the three as the invalid herself, another as her middle-aged caregiver, and the third as a young lawyer handling the dowager's estate.

To make functional and conceptual adjustments in a multilayered, stylized work like *Three Tall Women,* a playwright may need to confront his text on stage—alone or with cast and director. Routinely, at previews of his new plays, Albee stands at the back of the theatre, perhaps to see if viewers are catching his intentions on stage. If their reaction tells him a scene is not working, he may spot and correct the difficulty; to do so is more akin to "hearing" than to "pandering" to an audience. Hearing helps authors stage their intentions clearly during a script's performance-interpretations. In notes and comments over three decades, Albee has said that he makes these adjustments even though whatever play he puts down on paper "is usually complete before rehearsals."[3] Recently he stressed again his objectivity in adjusting texts: "I make one draft, and then a few penciled revisions, and then we make changes in rehearsal" (Brady 1994, 12). The effort puts the author's intentions with text and subtext clearly before his audiences.

That Albee had directed the play's initial production himself in Vienna was not atypical. Albee says, "I direct a lot of my plays first time around because I have a very clear vision of what I want" (Samuels 1994, 38). Vienna's audiences had received the play well, though its media reviews were mixed. Most critics knew that Albee's play was "still in progress" and looked forward to viewing it again (Kramar 1991, 36). In the months back in New York after its Vienna premiere, Albee further developed the play's material alone before taking a fresh look at it with Sacharow, who directed the next production "in consultation with Albee" at the 1992 Woodstock Festival (Pacheco 1994, 38). Albee has stated, albeit in a different context, "I am interested in finding out if there's a relationship between my view of [a play] and anyone else's" (Samuels 1994, 38). He and his director appear to have avoided subjective/objective conflicts in their approach to the staging—a virtual walk in the sunshine for both.

Albee has said that he and Sacharow worked very closely together, and that his own "clear vision" for *Three Tall Women* was "really not very different from what's on the stage now" (Samuels 1994, 38). Though the playwright gave Sacharow "a free hand" with the Woodstock production, the director and cast felt "the pressure of [the playwright's] presence" at rehearsals and conferences (Abramson 1992, 12). Albee gave the cast no notes directly; he talked to Sacharow, who relayed to the cast what he had indicated. Albee still added lines and made cuts while the play was "in an experimental stage" (Abramson 1992, 12). Sacharow and cast accepted the process as "proper and correct procedure when working on an Albee play" (Abramson 1992, 12). In years past, Albee has been one of theatre's most independent playwrights;[4] today, though he still gives no heed to critics' carping on his style or to popular calls for lighter drama, Sacharow and cast found him "the least dictatorial of authors, the most considerate and sensitive" in interactions with the company (Abramson 1992, 12). After Woodstock, Sacharow and Albee took the play to Manhattan in 1994. There, the Vineyard Theatre Company mounted it twice, first in lower Manhattan, then uptown at the Promenade Theatre, where it earned its author the Pulitzer Prize for 1994. It was a stroll in the limelight for cast and director as well.

From first to last venue, functional adjustments appeared in the setting—the bedroom of the play's invalid dowager. At Vienna's English Theatre, the room had been small yet elegant, its walls covered with blue moiré. Upholstered chairs, an end table, and a lamp furnished the room; a doorway at either side provided exits. Though at Woodstock Sacharow kept the set the same, at lower Manhattan's Vineyard Theater, he and designer James Noone adjusted it to the thrust-stage with audience on three sides. Uptown at the more spacious Promenade Theatre, they added alcoves at each side of the set to replace the simple doors; furnishings were more resplendent than before; an oversized bed and its coverings, brass lamps, and a sterling silver tea service reflected more appropriately the status of the invalid occupant.

While these functional shifts in setting required care by the director, an imposing factor in the text's basic structure needed a more drastic approach. At the work's first production in Vienna, Albee's text had required a conceptual leap by viewers from Act I's virtual realism to Act II's surrealistic realm. Unlike his popular play of the 1960s, *Who's Afraid of Virginia Woolf?*, which had observed most of drama's classical strictures on unity of time and situation, *Three Tall Women* abandons such formal limits. As a result, its broad periphery had been a hurdle to critics at Vienna. Yet it was only a challenge to be addressed at Woodstock and later venues after consultation between director Sacharow and playwright Albee. One critic at Vienna had called the play's form convoluted: "It forces us to figure out which of two worlds the playwright is drawing us into, the naturalistic world of Act I or the stylized world of Act Two" (Luere 1992, 251). When Albee brought up the lights on Vienna's Act II, the still-familiar faces of Act I's invalid, caregiver, and law clerk had startled viewers who, with consternation, heard the younger two actresses deliver lines disconnected from their previous roles. Two years later, canny adjustments by the team of Sacharow and Albee smoothed the transition from Act I's reality to Act II's fantasy. One clever shift in staging after Vienna made the actress playing the attendant walk with a stoop throughout Act I, then reenter with a straight spine and faster gait for her Act II identity as the middle-aged mother.

A second adjustment for viewers was the rethinking of the costuming for the actresses in Act II. The New York stagings linked the second act's surreal mothers to each other through harmoniously colored gowns and similar pearl necklaces. The actresses themselves, in interviews, spoke of the team's insightful, personal selection of their gowns for Act II (Abramson 1992, 12). This ploy subtly apprised viewers of a common thread joining the three; consequently, the audience, suspecting that the roles were now related in some new but slippery fashion, soon began to disconnect the women from their Act I moorings. Viewers were helped, too, by a more decided focusing of the characters' delivery of lines. A pronounced shift of personal pronouns occurred at the later venues as the two older figures warned the younger one of what was to come for her. Each addressed the younger with a sentence that used the second person "you will," yet in the same breath shifted to first person "I did." Soon we, like the young-mother component, saw their common identity when she admitted to them, "You have things to tell me, I suppose" (Albee, *Three Tall Women*, 47).

Viewers entered the stylized world of Act II more easily, too, when Sacharow delved into the subtext of Albee's play. The director brought up more of the majestic passion that, from the start, had been lurking in the playwright's pages (Canby 1994, sec. H, p. 5). Albee has referred in lectures to the importance of "subtext," of its "emotional coloring," of what he considers "implicit directions—those that are contained within the essence and nature of the character."[5] Soon, particularly in Act II, Sacharow helped the actresses "play the sense of their lines" (Canby 1994, sec. H, p. 5). Like Eugene O'Neill, who "turned to monologues, soliloquies, and asides for his characters' solitary outpourings," Albee had scripted intense emotions for the three women through soliloquies "not so much heard as overheard" (O'Neill 1967, xx). At the play's later stagings, Sacharow's pronounced reliance on Albee's subtext let us overhear Act II's fervent "private thoughts" more deeply or personally than three years before at Vienna; hence we noted more readily the overlaps in the women's tales and made swifter guesses at connections in their lives. We were, of course, still aware that here, as at Vienna, Albee had mystically altered these roles between acts without spelling it out for us. Yet now we could suspend rather quickly our disbelief in author magic that gave us a dowager lying on the bed while standing upright near the others. In the throes of similar bits of imposing fantasy, we still grasped Albee's intent: the commonality of the three roles. The playwright's intentions came across to both sides of the footlights when Sacharow's staging followed Albee's implicit "interpretive directions" (Syd M. 1992, 7); one critic has doubted that "cast and director ever deviate from his word" (Syd M. 1992, 7)—or "subtext," one can add.

Careful interchange between playwright and director also brought pivotal adjustments to the cast's delivery of text. Actresses at the Vienna production had handled monologues in an interesting presentational fashion—though Albee's customary preference has been for a far less stylized (but still direct) delivery of monologues. When the play moved from Vienna to New York, playwright, director, and actresses achieved a less rigid style. In the New York staging, one scene in particular displayed this shift in presentation. In Vienna, Albee's blocking had placed his youngest actress (Cynthia Bashard) downstage early in Act II, facing out over footlights to deliver a monologue on her naiveté as a girl. Her rhetorical skill would have earned high marks in a speech class. The actress, portraying the play's mother-figure at age twenty-six, took the audience into her confidence, ignoring the actresses playing the mother at age fifty-four (Kathleen Butler) and at ninety-two (Myra Carter). She might shift her body slightly to show her long gown swirling at a dance or fashion show. Yet her monologue had cued all audience attention directly on her while the other two actresses were decidedly out of the picture. Some Vienna reviewers, though drawn by *Three Tall Women*'s philosophical thrust, were not fond of these classic presentational modes (or were unfamiliar with them); they found the staging "stiff and confrontational . . . appropriate for statues" (Herles 1992, 12) and called the actresses' eloquent delivery "out-moded and wooden" (Kramar 1991, 36). One hopes the same critics saw the play again, a year or two later, when the scene's staging more closely reflected the playwright's intent; for at Woodstock, with Albee's and Sacharow's attention, the actress (Jordan Baker) adopted a less elocutionary tone, moved freely toward or away from the other women as she spoke. She included them as well as the audience in her account; they in turn reacted to her. By the time the play moved from Woodstock's River Arts to Manhattan's Vineyard Theater and then to the Promenade, Albee sanctioned even more movement for the scene while she delivered her lines (Albee, *Three Tall Women*, 47). When the actress (again, Jordan Baker) danced or modeled her gown, crossing the stage in large, graceful circles, the middle-span of Albee's mother-figure (Marian Seldes) moved a few feet behind her, equally gracefully, following her movements around the area, body-miming her. The scene became alive, pulsatingly theatrical, the effect one of movement rather than stasis, providing an engaging theatre picture.

Besides this softening of the style of presentation, more clarity and emphasis appeared through subtle shifts Albee made in the dialogue, forcefully staged by Sacharow. For the dowager, his shifts made her speech less pretentious and her mind more cluttered. In her conversation at Vienna, the aged invalid's use of the word "surcease" (to describe a letup in life's anxieties) had been ubiquitous. By Manhattan, however, "surcease" disappeared totally from her lines, replaced by more usual phrases for our release from life's pain: "when it's all done," or "when we can stop" (Albee, *Three Tall Women*, 47). Appropriately, from first to last production, Albee kept her language sexist, racist, but never sexually explicit. She might relate sensual anecdotes and indulge in crudities like "wop," "little Jew," and "coloreds" (44), yet she stayed with the innocent term "pee-pee" for her talk of men's genitals, and with the clipped "have to go" for her rush for the facilities (40, 46). The changes Albee made in her conversation at later stagings also accentuated her withdrawal of mind from body, her tendency to think of herself in the abstract (53)—one of Albee's motifs in works like *Marriage Play* and *Fragments*. As she more often lost track of her thoughts while sharing her past with the others on stage or across the footlights, we accepted her rambling and tied it to "the very familiar struggle of the aged with encroaching senility" (Brantley 1994, sec. C, p. 13). The naturalness of these scenes, re-scripted by Albee and well served by Sacharow, pulled at viewers who watched her degenerate.

Sacharow also added significant focus on the role of the fifty-four-year-old and on her catalogue of what parents should impart to offspring. At Vienna the audience heard her broad and sweeping prods on how we, as parents, fail in our duty to teach our children that they are not the center of the universe, nor are they owed a lifetime of happiness by being born. By Manhattan, the text seemed more jarring when this middle-aged figure recited her harangues: We heard her say that as children grow up, parents try "to hedge, to qualify, and to evade" the truth rather than give offspring the likely "alternatives to the 'pleasing prospects' " (Albee, *Three Tall Women*, 47). Whereas at Vienna she had advised us of the woeful weakness of men who would be our Prince Charmings, at Manhattan she emphasized details of their "sewer-rat morals" and warned that men at their club's stags "probably nail the whores to the billiard tables for easy access" (50). At these later productions, more vulgar and obscene language (from the "f" word to scatological terms) appeared, scattered throughout this middle-aged mother's lines (51, 53).

At Vienna, *Der Standard*'s Wolfgang Herles had thought the caretaker's portrait stereotyped: "It is as though Albee crossed Chekhov with the feminism found in women's entertainment magazines" (Herles 1992, 12). With Sacharow's added stage business at New York, the caregiver (Marian Seldes) jolted Act I's viewers with a bolder image than before. Seldes found new depth in Albee's intentions for this character, played her as "a hardened woman, stern in voice and appearance, yet with the slightest touch of softness to her—a rock with soft cream center" (Syd M. 1992, 7). The director, playwright, and actress had hardened the attendant's "center" to rock—or, if not her center, her back; for, as noted earlier, she came on stage stiff and forward-slanted, and with a strident voice that exposes her "attitude" toward her aged employer. At Vienna, though she had registered irritation at her invalid-charge by a sigh or roll of her eyes, she had quickly regained her humor. In contrast, the Manhattan staging allowed less comic relief on her face as she complains of the boring rituals of sick-care. (Her repeated comment about the monotony and frustrations of her daily lot, "And so it goes," was Albee's first title for the play [Albee, *Three Tall Women*, 41, 42, 47, 52, 53].) Even with the hardening of the caregiver's stance and language, Manhattan audiences remained empathetic toward her—as only two of Vienna's critics had been (Zamponi 1991, 37; Luere 1992, 252). New York's reviewers, night after night for weeks thereafter, called Marian Seldes's performance stunning, "droll and delightful," Myra Carter's "huge" and "heroic," and broadcast the word that their performances were the most riveting in town.[6]

The role of the youngest of the play's three women also grew with Albee and Sacharow during the play's journey. At Vienna, the staging had made the actress (Cynthia Bashard) seem ingenuous as she told of her first sexual encounter; at a dance, her shy eyes and hesitant tone had shown surprise and distress to feel her partner's body pressing hers. By Woodstock, the director and playwright team parlayed a shift in staging, and the actress (now, Jordan Baker) delivered the same tale with calculation—less faltering and more design. Then, at the ultimate New York stagings, even more sensuality and less innocence surfaced (Albee, *Three Tall Women*, 47–48). Viewers heard the actress repeat the same lines with sophistication, with pride on her face and delight in her voice, and noted a swaying of her hips as she reveled in her sexuality. (Has Albee given us a Martha-in-the-making?)

Sacharow's attention to the actress's demeanor elsewhere in the play had also, by Woodstock, given her decided bluntness and over-confidence. At Vienna, Albee had called for her to be a bit insensitive toward the invalid's disintegration and to contradict her on occasion; by Woodstock and Manhattan, reviewers sensed an increase in the young clerk's callousness (Canby 1994, sec. H, p. 5; Brantley 1994, sec. C, p. 13). She followed her ridicule of the old one's sexist or racist comments with snide "under-the-breath" replies of "Jesus!" or "Jesus Christ!" and was so rude to her that, ashamed of herself, she asked contritely, "Why can't I be nice? (Albee, *Three Tall Women*, 40, 42, 44). Yet when the tired and pained old invalid spoke with a whine (Albee, *Three Tall Women*, 45), the young one's voice still remained shrill and sarcastic. Here, Albee's preoccupation with sound—with tone of voice—parallels that of Samuel Beckett, who called his own work "a matter of sounds."[7] Director Sacharow suggests that Albee's interest in sound, particularly the tones of the human voice, developed from his love of opera; he finds the playwright's indications for tone as precise as musical notations (Abramson 1992, 12). Playing the concisely drawn role with zest, Jordan Baker, like Seldes and Carter, soon collared media attention;[8] with Albee's multidimensional depiction of all three characters, the columns of the *New York Times, Theater Week, Playbill, Time, Newsweek,* and *Parade,* again without exception, praised the Pulitzer committee's choice of *Three Tall Women* for its 1994 award.[9]

Equally effective was the consultation of Sacharow with Albee on the play's ancillary mystical figure—the dowager's estranged and prodigal son, who materializes midway into Act II. Through this character, the brilliant script examines classic ruptures in mother-son relationships. At Vienna, Albee had centered on the son (Howard Nightengall) but slightly. Its blocking brought the actor briskly on stage to step to the sickbed where a surreal figure lay with oxygen mask covering nose and mouth. The son had leaned to kiss the figure's hands, then remained briefly by the bed, attentive to the figure though aware of three women standing apart. After a time, he had unobtrusively exited. Though the script did not specify how long the actor would remain on stage or if he would exit at all (Albee, *Three Tall Women*, 53), at later venues Albee and Sacharow kept him omnipresent throughout more of the scene, with lighting and blocking imprinting him on viewers' consciousness. By Manhattan, the son (Michael Rhodes) strode across the large room, attended to the figure on the bed, but at times stepped a few inches away to move for a moment toward the three (52, 53), where his presence pierced the audience as he stared at each of the virtually real onlookers. As the son heard the midlife mother blast at his past conduct and order him to leave, he shuddered; when the oldest approached, he reached to touch her though she shrank from him (52). Sacharow's blocking let us see his face more sharply than at earlier stagings, and we hoped he'd reach out again, would say "I'm sorry. . . . I've come back!"[10] Yet the sensitive script kept him wordless—what words could suffice? We know that in the real world the son did come back, bringing freesia and candied orange peel, her favorites, and seeing to happy hours for her. Yet at all venues, Albee's theatre world kept him silent. Was Manhattan's staging meant to heighten our awareness of a son's love, or of his sting— of a mother's pain, or outrage? The author's bent for ambivalence lets us choose.

Viewers who had caught *Three Tall Women* from Vienna to Manhattan noted a particular gain from Sacharow's and Albee's consultation over the final scene. The playwright's vision for *Three Tall Women* from the start seemed to have been that the dowager's threefold nature was as real for her as for us. Albee has said in another recent play that our younger selves "always stay with us—lurk around the edges of our consciousness" (Albee, *The Lorca Play*, 4). At Vienna, however, Albee's blocking of the last scene had guaranteed that the self-absorbed invalid herself, alone, would hold the audience with her irony-filled monologue on what the end of life's misery—surcease—had brought her. That staging had locked our minds on what a woman in her dotage was preaching to us: Joy comes only after strife (Richards 1991, sec. 2, p. 19)—although one critic commented that "when and where the truly happy moments of life are is left a question by the author" (Shine 1992, sec. 2, p. 7). Albee may hint at an answer to the "when and where" at the Vineyard-Promenade

America's first Elizabethan Stage. Based on the Fortune Theatre Contract, by designer Richard Hay, for the Oregon Shakespeare Festival, Ashland, Oregon. Courtesy of Glenn M. Loney.

Lawrence Sacharow, director of Edward Albee's Pulitzer Prize winning play, *Three Tall Women*. Photo: Carol Rosegg. Used by permission.

The cast of *Three Tall Women*: Nan Martin, Kathleen Butler, and Tracy Sallows in the 1995 Alley Theatre (Houston) production, directed by Lawrence Sacharow. Photo: Carol Rosegg. Used by permission.

Playwright Edward Albee. Photo: Susan Johann. Used by permission.

Scene from Edward Albee's *The Lorca Play*. Photo: Houston Chronicle. Used by permission.

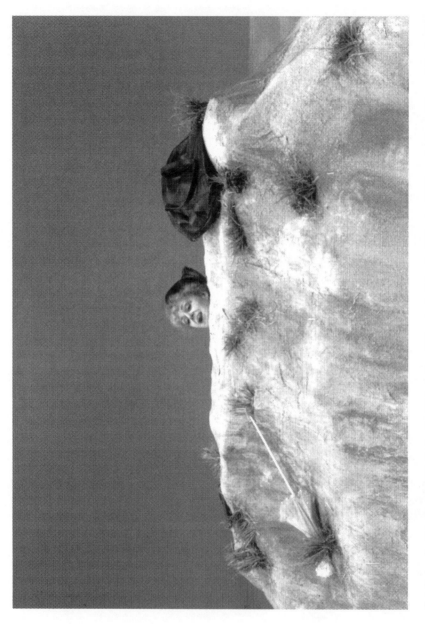

Set design by Jonathan Middents for the University of Houston's School of Theatre 1993 production of Samuel Beckett's *Happy Days*, with Patricia Kilgarriff. Courtesy of University of Houston, School of Theatre.

where he and director Sacharow blocked the three women in a striking triptych downstage. The actresses' arms were linked and their hands clasped. Sacharow's triptych blocking helped us reconsider each of the three, close yet separate, not the elder alone, whereupon we marveled at the slices of life that remain with the dowager. One might say that Manhattan's finish, rather than simply pointing out "Ah, the lady's wise!" made us ponder the how-when-where of her seasoning. This wisdom accrued from a reconsideration of three discrete selves locked into her being. The interpretation of this stylized final scene by director and actors was a credit to the playwright's striking text.

In sum, mystery shrouds our perception of minds that create art of this caliber. A crystal moment may account for the dawn of a masterpiece. Edward Albee says, "I find that I am with play."[11] Yet after that dawning, a full measure of objectivity—his and his director's—undoubtedly makes the text a theatrical experience. Manuscripts, letters, and diaries, both of literary giants and their directors, suggest this reality. Asked if he "rewrites," Albee will joke, "I don't make notes for posterity" (Samuels 1994, 38). Does it matter? What we see is that after a play's gestation inside the creative mind, authors want to be close to their texts during a director's interpretation. After all, theatre history doesn't say that Shakespeare dropped off a manuscript at the Globe and disappeared. Albee, too, has stayed by his scripts—alone or with a trusted director from Alan Schneider to Lawrence Sacharow.

MICHAEL WILSON: 1995 DIRECTION OF *ANGELS IN AMERICA* AT THE ALLEY THEATRE'S ARENA STAGE

A decision to stage a recent Pulitzer Prize–winning play might give any director qualms at the start. Previous productions, hailed and reviewed at resident theatres here and in thirty-two countries abroad, could suggest precedents to follow—or to avoid if a director and his team hoped to keep their own intentions fresh and distinctive.

At Houston's Alley Theatre in 1995, when director Michael Wilson was thinking of tackling Tony Kushner's two-part, seven-hour period piece, *Angels in America*, the play's press reviews for its 1993 staging were still widely circulating. Besides its Pulitzer, the play, developed in 1992 at Los Angeles' Mark Taper Forum, had already received the 1993 and 1994 Tony Awards, the 1993 and 1994 Drama Desk Award, two Olivier Awards, the London *Evening Standard* Award, and the London Drama Circle Critics' Award. Hence director Wilson may have viewed circumspectly his chances for an inventive staging of a play already "a watershed in American Theatre" (Weeks 1995, sec. D, p. 7).

Wilson need not have been anxious; both Part I: *Millennium Approaches* and Part II: *Perestroika*, directed by Wilson at the Alley in rotating repertory, drew positive critical and popular reaction. Audiences applauded the freshness of the production and the contemporary relevance of Kushner's epic on life in AIDS-beset America. Houston critics said Wilson's production had a "white-hot brilliance" (Everett Evans 1995, "Perestroika," 10). Wilson's direction placed on the Alley Stage an artistic performance that was distinctive and inventive besides reflecting "the wit, grace, and humanity" critics had lauded in the New York production (Davidson, quoted in Weeks 1995, sec D, p. 7).

Wilson's decision to stage the play had tested the resourcefulness of director and theatre staff during planning, for the play would be performed, not on a proscenium stage like its Broadway premiere, but on a small arena stage. Yet the reach of the script was astounding in social and philosophical reflections on America. Set in the 1980s in the Reagan–Bush era and billed as a "Gay Fantasia on American Themes," it touched our nation's factional makeup. The content, Kushner has suggested, "explores alternatives to individualism and the political economy it serves" (Kushner 1993, 31). Scholar-critic David Savran, reviewing one 1993 staging, had found in the work "two strands of Utopian thinking: early Mormonism and the Marxism of Walter Benjamin" (quoted in *Chronicles of Higher Education* [23 June 1995], sec. A, p. 11). At the Alley, the director, his actors, and designers all involved themselves in a team attack on the complex script to ensure a smash performance. Kushner has often said that the nature of drama is collaborative and calls it a fiction that "artistic accomplishment is exclusively the provenance of individual talents" or "that artistic labor happens in isolation" (Kushner 1993, 1). Wilson's broad experience as playwright, actor, and director gave his fellow artists at the Alley an edge on interpreting and staging the playscript.

Wilson and his staff for *Angels in America* must have been physically taxed by the script's large cast of sixteen characters played by eight actors, its elaborate scenic and lighting demands, and its mixture of reality and fantasy. The fast-paced script orders actors to go and come between Earth and Heaven as the playwright attacks sexual and social problems and berates humanity for shifting between progress and stasis in its attempts to correct weaknesses. The characters' lives are interrelated; they mix hallucinations and dreams into their conversations about their dilemmas.

With Wilson's experience in directing, Alley actors met the script's challenges and showed us distinctly each character's troubled consciousness. Prior Walter (played by John Feltch), a gay man with AIDS, is badgered by reactionary angels who want him to serve as a prophet to help mankind return to earlier, supposedly more moral and ethical behavior. (Critics comment that the playwright himself, a thirty-nine-year-old New Yorker, may now have become the "prophet"—the new voice of American Theatre, pushing against stasis [Weeks 1995, sec. 7, p. D].)

Louis Ironson (Joseph Haj) is Walter's Jewish lover, and Belize (Michael McElroy) is Prior Walter's cross-dressing nurse. Joe Pitt (David Whalen) is a Mormon lawyer and closeted gay, whose wife Harper (Annalee Jefferies) lives on valium, moving in and out of hallucinations. Roy Cohn (James Black), crony of that era's infamous Joseph McCarthy, is fatally ill yet still clutching at political power. Wilson's clever direction of these characters and a bevy of others—some human; some angels; plus one shade, Ethel Rosenberg (Bettye Fitzpatrick)—made them strikingly convincing in multiple roles.

The script's action starts in 1985 in New York City, shifts to Moscow in 1986, and includes a trip to Heaven for an Angels Conference on the need for human beings' concerted resistance to their culture's unwholesome status quo. Wilson's firm direction provides coherence in these shifting settings. The angels confer on how to persuade earthlings to get off their daily treadmills and return to a more conservative culture-epoch before the 1980s. The play looks closely at love, politics, death, and redemption, asking questions about the link between moral and spiritual death and sexual politics. Characters discuss the fall of Marxist theory and the rise of America's capitalism but appear to dismiss "revolution in the Marxist sense" as "virtually unthinkable" (Savran, quoted in *Chronicles of Higher Education* [23 June 1995], sec. A, p. 11). The audience sees the characters' frailty and disenchantment as their interconnected stories unfold. The play's action ends with the characters back in New York City, sitting pensively in Central Park near the Bethesda Fountain.

Wilson's choice—to mount the play at the Alley's Neuhaus Arena Stage—must have given his designers, Tony Straiges and Kenneth Posner, both breaks and drawbacks. However Kushner, the playwright, had asked that the play be presented on an arena stage. Though the designers would have known from the outset that an arena stage was a boon for the audience, ensuring a feeling of intimacy, pulling the audience toward the actors and their entwined lives, it would also be a hurdle for them with its lack of sophisticated, intricate machinery that large New York venues could employ to fly the actors between Earth and more atmospheric areas. At the Alley, working with simple, hand-maneuvered mechanisms, Wilson and his team still gave the audience the feeling that shimmering wings of angels were rising and descending among the human characters with dispatch—though they saw, of course, the simple poles and platforms by which stagehands moved them. The designers had mapped and tested these operations so well that we readily accepted the ups and downs of the actors. Also effective were projections from high screens hanging at corners of the stage, planned by designer Jeff Cowie to add dimension to the scenes through close-ups of relevant faces and related places. These protruding images helped viewers bind people to events in Wilson's fast-paced scenes.

Wilson's direction of his eight actors in multiple roles took them smoothly through the script's physical challenges; the actors executed stage business smoothly, hopping in, out, and under hospital beds; carting luggage while wending their way through NYC's suburbs; hiding medical supplies here and there; taking part in involved dioramas at a Mormon Visitors' Center. Actor James Black played his character (Roy Cohn) as a man in denial, raging in his sickbed, using former cronies to retain his political power. The script required Black's character to argue heatedly with his compassionate nurse Belize (Michael McElroy) over bootlegged medication that he hoped could prolong Cohn's life. As Prior Walter, John Feltch's wrestling match with the chief of the angels (acted by Shelly Williams) was a shocker. Staged convincingly by Wilson's movement coach, Mark Olsen, it startled the audience with its outcome—an angel, down but not out—and made us dismiss the absurdity of the fight itself.

Although these disputes and physical struggles made strong stage pictures, the director focused more often on the emotional strength of Kushner's characters amid society's crumbling foundations in the 1980s. Their culture-epoch faced failures in the human body's protective systems, depletion in our planet's ozone, and mishaps in our constitution's basic guarantees. Wilson's well-directed actors depicted the maturation their characters achieved experientially over the threatening decade Kushner's script condenses into seven hours of stage time. As the play progressed, the actors helped the audience hope that the betrayed wife, Harper (Annalee Jefferies), would be able to live fully on her own without Joe, her mixed-up husband, and that Prior Walter would be savvy enough to dodge all further intrusions by angels. Especially encouraging was the swing toward compassion of Joe's Mormon mother, who had hoped to see her son "get well"—as she calls it—from his gay bent.

The smooth communication between Wilson and his costume designer, Caryn Neman, helped the actors project their roles to the audience. Belize (Michael McElroy), who does "drag," looked his part in the glitzy garb designed for him by Neman. The staid business suits of Joe Pitt (David Whalen) as the inhibited but bisexual Mormon instantly spoke to us of the character's initial discomfort in the arms of gay Louis. The actor's ultraconservative look convinced us, too, that before his character's gay sprint, he could well have written far-right tracts for Cohn, his McCarthyite boss. And costumer Neman's skill did not let us miss the flakiness of Harper (Annalee Jefferies), wrapping her in blanketlike clothes that played up her imbalance and lack of self-image. When her attire changed to "svelte" much later, the switch let us hope Harper would regain her esteem and her will to live. Neman's choice of attire for Prior Walter (John Feltch)—a long cape and hood—gave him an appropriate monklike look, thoughtful and serene, when his character seemed to accept his angel-appointed role of prophet. Later, when he seemed to receive the gift of grace—a bit more life—his sprightly clothing matched his lighter demeanor and supplied us with hope that he would make some progress in his and his friends' way of living.

These designers and actors, like their director, obviously grasped the playwright's intent and worked with the director to reflect the play's thematic concerns in performance. Kushner's characterization and dramatic action push the concept that our basic drive as humans is to move forward—though change is both difficult and painful. Actress Bettye Fitzpatrick, who played five roles in the play, has said, "The importance of Tony Kushner's message makes it a joy to work on this script"; and John Feltch, playing Prior Walter, called the whole cast "well-rehearsed" and their effort "an amazing achievement" (Everett Evans 1995, "The Work of 'Angels,' " 12).

Indisputably, Michael Wilson and his company kept the magic, the outlandish connections, and the poetry of Kushner's script as they brought to the stage the playwright's philosophy espoused through his characters: that thoughtful people want "more life" rather than easy ends to troubled existence (Kushner 1993, 30). After all, Kushner's Prior Walter chose to keep on, to climb down the ladder from Heaven to Earth. The characters in the play are moving toward their futures. In an article published with the text of *Angels in America*, Kushner said, "More life is the key to the heart of *Perestroika*" (31). Kushner and his characters may look for "paths of resistance," but they seek, too, for "pockets of peace, and places from whence hope may be plausibly expected" (31). At the Alley, the experience and sensitivity of director Wilson and his actors' fine delivery of roles sent home with audiences this urge toward hope and forward movement.

MARTIN PLATT AND RICHARD ROSENBERG: SENDING AN ADAPTATION BACK TOWARD ITS SOURCE— *CARMEN* FROM 1838 TO 1995

Bravo for directors who can cope with adaptations. For one director to reproduce another director's "adaptation" of a classic is a risky venture: In essence, one would be "imitating an imitation" rather than pursuing a challenge on his own.

The coping can be doubly trying in musical theatre, where performance may involve both a director and a musical director. At Santa Fe Stages in 1995, director Martin L. Platt and musical director Richard Rosenberg performed English stage director Peter Brook's *La Tragédie de Carmen* (a 1981 adaptation of Georges Bizet's 1838 *Carmen*). The Santa Fe staging of Brook's celebrated work was unique, for Platt and Rosenberg were determined to take as their point of departure many original indications of the Bizet opera that Brook had dropped.

Some critics have considered Brook "a theatrical magician" (Giffin 1995, sec. E, p. 7). Others say he reduces "panoramas to microcosms" (Holland 1995, sec. C, p. 14). Directors Platt and Rosenberg deemed Brook's score "only the bare bones" of Bizet's plot and music, yet rife with possibilities (Giffin 1995, sec. E, p. 7). Brook, in 1981, had waved his wand at Bizet's century-old *Carmen* to redistribute arias, rearrange scenes, and remove many roles. The changes Brook made in Bizet's original were "essentially a shaving off of all the extraneous choruses—the children, the gypsies, cigar girls, Escamillo's entourage, leaving us with Carmen, Don Jose, Escamillo, and Micaela—Bizet's primary cast" (Rosenberg, quoted in Giffin 1995, sec. E, p. 7). Brook's designer, Marius Constant, had helped him develop his musical adaptation, which shrank the source to eighty minutes, omitted the brilliant overture, added music for continuity, cut the orchestral score to fifteen musicians (in effect, a chamber orchestra), and shifted its tempo. Platt's and Rosenberg's challenge was to give the Brook's adaptation and its Santa Fe audience more of the sensory impact of Bizet's original.

Music director Rosenberg's early, firsthand experience had been with organizations whose work required full textual respect for composers. His performance background included positions with the London Classical Band and the London Classical Players, ensembles noted for historically informed performances using classical techniques and original instruments. Other theatre figures have, like Platt and Rosenberg, been attracted by innovations of author-directors like Peter Brook. The terms "enhancement," "adaptation," and "transformation" often appear in their discussions both of dramatic and of musical literature, addressing the amount of adherence to text a specific author-director demonstrates. Playwright-director Edward Albee, who has staged four of Samuel Beckett's plays, states precisely his own position on primacy of text: "With a play that wants its text respected, respect its text; with a play that is a set of improvisations or that approaches theater from a totally different point of view, then do it that way. I've never thought anything was the wave of the future except possibly diversity."[1] Peter Brook has often declared his own liberal stance on textual ethics—on opportunities and responsibilities of directors who modify established scripts and scores. In an Introduction to Peter Weiss's (1965) *Marat/Sade*, Brook explained that staging should "stir our perceptions" of a manuscript by observing the "sounds and ideas, thoughts, images" that the composer of the score has "crammed into each instant" (Brook 1965, v). Yet Sucher, in 1995's "All the Rest Is Chatter," revealed that Brook's aesthetic for adaptations included a ceaseless urge to cut from a script or score whatever, in his judgment, is not essential. His transformations "make a stage barer and more stark, reduce scenery and equipment" (Sucher 1995, 18). Why? Brook felt that "In theater, if you use everything, the whole technique, if everything is visible, you reach, very quickly, I think, the border of banality" (Brook 18). Still, how much an inventive director's subjectivity might affect an author's scripted "instants" may perplex staunch supporters of textual primacy.

Concerns over concepts of "adaptation" and "rendition" were quite familiar to directors Platt and Rosenberg when they began rehearsals for Brook's *La Tragédie de Carmen* at the Santa Fe Stages. They were aware, as many theatre fans have been, of the roundabout route the work had already taken on its way to Bizet before Brook approached it in the 1980s. Bizet's *Carmen*, like many masterworks then and now, had its own ancestor—a novella about a very different Don Jose, written by Prosper Mérimée (1803–1870), French novelist, archeologist, and historian of Bizet's century.[2] Details like these tease writers who expect total respect for text in theatre. In bringing a play to its audience, however, the legal responsibilities and interactions of producers or directors like Bizet (or Brook) vary with the time, intent, and extent of modification. Directors Platt and Rosenberg knew that Bizet's borrowing in 1881 from an author of his own period—Mérimée—had been within bounds of propriety because Bizet appropriated the material for a different genre—opera, not fiction. They were also aware that Brook, in 1981, could freely follow his own voice in shaving *Carmen* because Bizet's death had occurred a century earlier. Though Brook's version retained Bizet's four principals, the adaptation redistributed Bizet's music among them and assigned it different functions and weights in the story line. To Micaela, the second feminine role, he gave a duet with Carmen, one that in Bizet's opera Carmen had sung alone. And though Brook's Escamillo sings the same songs as he had for Bizet, Brook crowded the numbers into one scene that seemed like "a small, intense, black-and-white drawing" in place of *Carmen*'s large, brilliantly lit stage picture (Holland 1995, sec. C, p. 14). One critic called Brook's version "a throw-away in a bar" rather than "a big number on the glories of the bullfight" (Rosenberg, quoted in Giffin 1995, sec. E, p. 7).

Platt's and Rosenbloom's staging of Brook, with Bizet its point of departure, was less a reproduction of an adaptation and more an artistic challenge of Brook's innovations than most contemporary mountings of the work. One production, by a Manhattan theatre company in 1995, had followed the Brook score closely. Its staging, at the Mannes College of Music in Manhattan, led to comments that whatever "help" Brook may have given the "sprawling, drama-defying dialogue" of the Bizet original, the gift was at too great a price (Holland 1995, sec. C, p. 14). Critics had rued the Manhattan group's apparent "lack of all contact with Bizet's score" (Holland 1995, sec. C, p. 14). The company of Platt and Rosenberg were the antithesis, having followed a predilection for textual primacy. From the beginning of the project, their whole theatre team had sought guidance for their performance by recourse to the past. The directors and staff—choreographer Maria Benitez, scenic designer Russell Parkman, and lighting designer Peter Maradudin—researched records from the period of Bizet's composition of *Carmen* looking for "blood-in-the-sand" indications of performance tempo and style. The group began by following the unearthed indications literally and then "amended as necessary to accommodate the drama" (Rosenberg, quoted in Giffin 1995, sec. E, p. 7). Before the production at Santa Fe, their anticipation of the effect of their research on the audience shone in Rosenberg's statement: "What I think will be heard is probably closer to Bizet's intentions"—than to Brook's, he implied (quoted in Giffin 1995, sec. E, p. 7).

The company's integrity in looking back to a source, though appropriate, could seem a whit short to authors who want their texts totally respected; and the need to look back might itself seem a bit ironic to adapters of Brook's type in a culture that pushes for innovation and improvisation. We need a clearer policy on primacy of text. To authors whose works are appropriated, some comfort might come if they grant that the "best" is often the most copied, adapted, embellished—all with excellent intent. A century ago, Giuseppe Verdi's aim was sincere with his 1887 opera via Shakespeare's 1604 tragedy, *Othello*. Verdi had convinced himself that "[by] simplifying Shakespeare's plot and character, by ignoring the complexity of Shakespeare's presentation of Desdemona and Othello, and by obliterating words and phrases and lines, indeed, by cutting a whole unnecessary first act," he was still "being true to Shakespeare's ultimate vision" (Swanston 1994, 8–10). Shakespeare's own indebtedness to *Othello*'s primary source, Giraldi Cinthio's 1565 novel, shows the playwright, in part, heeding the counsel of his time—that writers of tragedy would do well to use plots from contemporary culture.[3]

In our century's theatre, semantic tussles over text still surface wherever theatre figures meet to discuss innovation or, at more peril, deconstruction. Author-director-designer Robert Wilson, who, like Peter Brook, is known for his adaptations of classics, took part in a 1993 symposium at Houston's Alley Theatre, where questions on text emerged. Because Wilson's production of Wagner's *Parsifal* was scheduled for the new season, panelists were grilling Wilson about his controversial staging of the established classic in Hamburg two years before. One of the panelists, Edward Albee, commended Wilson's productions in general as "some of the most interesting theatrical experiences I've come across in the past twenty years" (quoted in Luere and Berger 1994, 21). It might be noted that not every Wilson adaptation has been well received; one, his deconstructed *Hamlet*, was largely unsuccessful. As others at the Alley Symposium sought background information on the upcoming production, Albee asked Wilson frankly: "This is not an improvisation on *Par-*

sifal or cuts from *Parsifal*—it's *Parsifal?*" To which Wilson answered, "It's *Parsifal*" (quoted in Luere and Berger 1994, 22). Albee replied, "Thank heavens," and Wilson assured him, "We have no cuts" (quoted in Luere and Berger 1994, 24). Recapping his work with *Parsifal*, Wilson told the group, "My production is different from any other that has been done in the history of *Parsifal*" (quoted in Luere and Berger 1994, 22). Of his Hamburg production, he said, "I felt it had very much respect for the text, the audio text and the music. . . . I tried to create a visual book around it that would reinforce it, support it, give us space so we can hear and see" (quoted in Luere and Berger 1994, 25).

Though Platt and Rosenberg, with Brook's adaptation of *Carmen*, had less of Bizet to weigh than Wilson had of Wagner, their anticipation of viewer response to their staging of Brook's *La Tragédie de Carmen* was as direct and positive as Wilson's for *Parsifal*. Music director Rosenberg said, "I don't think anyone can walk away without being deeply affected by what they've seen and heard" (quoted in Giffin 1995, sec. E, p. 7).

Audiences, critics, and other theatre folk enjoy without puzzlement the theatrical experiences offered by Peter Brook, Robert Wilson, and Giuseppe Verdi, especially when directors like Martin Platt and Richard Rosenberg stage them grounded in their sources' "scripted instants" (Brook 1965, vi). With Platt and Rosenberg, the term "scripted instants" may cover a tad more text than adaptations sometimes do.

NOTES

Director Lawrence Sacharow

1. In two critical volumes, Matthew C. Roudané discusses Albee's thrust of nontraditional theatre at audiences. *Public Issues, Private Tensions: Contemporary American Drama* (New York: AMS Press, 1993) and *Who's Afraid of Virginia Woolf?: Necessary Fictions, Terrifying Realities* (New York: G. K. Hall, 1990). See also his review of *The Man Who Had Three Arms* in *Modern Critical Views: Edward Albee*, Harold Bloom, ed. (New York: Chelsea House Publishers, 1987), 163.

2. For example, the van driver in *American Dream*, the mythical son in *Who's Afraid of Virginia Woolf?*, or Alice/Miss Alice in *Tiny Alice*.

3. At a forum in 1992, Albee said, "When I write a play on paper, I have spent a lot of time with it in my mind; and I know what it looks like and sounds like as a performed stage piece. So I see it as I write it as a piece which is performed by actors on a stage in front of an audience. . . . I claim that my plays don't change very much in rehearsal; I lie a little when I say that. I cut my plays because I overwrite—I get infatuated with the sound of my own voice and I put in all sorts of scenes and speeches that I am very fond of and that I will probably use in another play if I take them out of the play that they are in." (Reprinted from Luere and Berger, eds., *Playwright versus Director*, p. 24.)

4. Philip C. Kolin, ed., "Edward Albee in Conversation with Terrence Mc-

Nally," in *Conversations with Edward Albee* (Jackson and London: University of Mississippi Press, 1988), 207. See also Albee's comment on rewriting on the basis of critics' suggestions: "I don't believe in second guessing myself," James Brady, "In Step with Edward Albee," 12.

5. At seminars, Albee has spoken of the "emotional coloring in a text," found in an author's "implicit directions," which are "contained within the essence and nature of each character." Of emotion, Albee stresses that "The GOOD director translates what is already there in the play; he does not have to create [emotion] in a first-rate play. It's in the subtext" (Luere and Berger, eds., 50).

6. "Around Town," *New Yorker* (5 September 1994), 14. Also, from the *Woodstock Times* review (6 August 1992) calling the play a "Premier Premiere," to the *New York Times* coverage (14 February 1994) vowing that "Edward Albee Conjures Up Three Ages of Woman," major media reviewers lauded the performances of Myra Carter and Marian Seldes; Carter had played her role from Vienna through Woodstock and on to the Promenade, Seldes from Woodstock on. The third actress, Jordan Baker, who had joined the cast in Woodstock and received mixed reviews, won high praise for her acting at the Vineyard and the Promenade.

7. The passage on sound (in Beckett's letter of December 29, 1957 to Alan Schneider) follows: "My work is a matter of fundamental sounds (no joke intended) made as fully as possible, and I accept responsibility for nothing else. If people want to have headaches among the overtones, let them. And provide their own aspirin." "*Not I*: Beckett's Mouth and the Ars(e) Rhetorica." In Enoch Brater, ed., *Beckett at 80/Beckett in Context* (New York and Oxford: Oxford University Press, 1986), 124.

8. Syd M., in "Premier Premiere," writes that Baker "holds her own against these sterling actresses" (7).

9. Typical national news columns began with references like that in United Press's *Parade* insert (14 August 1994), p. 12, entitled "In Step with Edward Albee" by James Brady: "The Pulitzer Prize is the most prestigious award for writing; playwright Edward Albee has three Pulitzers, the most current award this spring for his current play, *Three Tall Women*."

10. At all stagings of *Three Tall Women*, the young man's role remained a silent one; audiences learn of the boy's kindness to the mother from her remarks earlier in the play.

11. When Mr. Albee was asked how he conceives a play, he said, "How does the material come? I don't know. All of a sudden I discover that I have been thinking about a play" (Kolin, ed., 22). Also, Mr. Albee's comment, "I find I am with play," recorded in class session at School of Theater, University of Houston, 20 April 1992, and in lecture at Michener Hall, University of Northern Colorado, Greeley, Colorado, 10 March 1983.

Martin Platt and Richard Rosenberg

1. Transcript of "Alley Forum," in Jeane Luere and Sidney Berger, eds., *Playwright versus Director* (London and New York: Greenwood Press, 1994), 22.

2. The characterization and style in Bizet's *Carmen* were wholly unlike those

of novelist Mérimée. Bizet, for his opera, had transformed Mérimée's male character, a common thug avoiding the law, into a romantic hero—Don Jose. He had
used the novella's gypsy girl as his Carmen, then asked his writers, Meilhac and
Halevy, to create an additional feminine role (Micaela) as a contrast to Carmen
(Giffin 1995, sec. E, p. 7).

3. In truth, Shakespeare followed his own voice by letting the moral of Cinthio's story crumble (G. Blakemore Evans, *The Riverside Shakespeare* [Boston:
Houghton Mifflin, 1974], 1198).

PART III
THE PLAYWRIGHT

8

The Playwright's Role

Oh, dramatists, the true applause which you seek is not the hand-
clapping; it is rather that profound sigh which escapes from the
depths of the [viewer's] soul after the constraint of long silence, the
sigh that brings relief. [Yet] another impression to make, a more violent one . . . is to make your audience feel ill at ease.

—Denis Diderot

Playwrights, like artists, "make the most of the idea that an observer
can participate in a pictured experience." . . . The purpose of art is to
"involve the viewer in it physically." Hence the dramatist "must not
allow us to pass by without noticing the turmoil, the upset," then
reacting to it "in shocked awareness."

—John Canaday

THE PLAYWRIGHT: SPRING, HEAD, AND FOUNTAIN
OF DRAMA

The playwright may seem to be a singularly independent artist who
works alone. To preserve his thoughts and visions in language, he picks
his own words, chooses his own style, and when he is ready, calls his
work complete. The play that results is his!

This supposition that "artistic accomplishment is exclusively the provenance of individual talent" has been challenged by contemporary playwrights (Kushner 1993, 1). Tony Kushner asks, "Is It a Fiction That
Playwrights Create Alone?" (Kushner 1993, 1). Edward Albee has said,

"I have been influenced by everything I have read . . . from Socrates to Noel Coward" (quoted in Kolin 1988, 30). To be "influenced" is not a derisive term that denies a writer's originality and genius; rather, "to be influenced" shows the breadth of one's reading and listening, participation and comprehension.

From another perspective, the notion that a playwright begets theatre alone slights the tie between text and staging. The moment a producer espies a script's potential, the playwright may become senior member and source of a production team. From that point on, a collaborative effort begins. In the best of life's scenarios, a director, designers, and actors will approach the script to construe the authorial vision concretely on a stage (Klaus, Gilbert, and Field 1991, 742). As dramatist Albee has written, "The playwriting craft is enormously imprecise since it has to be filtered through other people" (Kolin 1988, 33). Producer/composer Richard Rodgers (1978) wrote that theatre is never produced "by a single person" (306). Though on one night a play's premiere opens successfully, "It's because one, two, three or more people sat down and sweated over an idea that somehow clicked and broke loose" (Rodgers 1978, 327). The dedicated, concentrated effort by all who help the script "click and break loose" testifies to the playwright-creator's genius.

The sense and the sagacity of our top dramatists have enabled them to fulfill what theatre history hails as drama's ultimate purpose: to capture and to stir our theatre audiences. The audience will respond if the theatre team scrutinizes the script to find the "sounds and ideas, lights, images" that master playwrights "cram into each instant" (Brook 1965, 18). When lucky theatre audiences absorb the team's splendidly staged moments from their seats, the playwright's work becomes unforgettable. Even in the first half of our century, theatre figures like Antonin Artaud (1896–1948) thought drama's business was to break down our minds' defenses—what psychology today calls our "denials." Too often our minds have been "conditioned to sublimate many human impulses and to sell out to conformity" (Artaud 1958, 31). Good playwrights vow that "at its best, theatre is an argument against the status quo. A serious play always holds a mirror up to people and says, 'Look, this is who you are. This is how you behave. If you don't like it, why don't you change?' " (Albee 1995, Press Club Transcript 7). Playwrights help us "drain abscesses collectively" (Artaud 1958, 31). The consequence can be our gain in emotional openness.

This particular role of playwrights—to "provoke society into facing its shortcomings" (Brockett 1982, 681)—has led many playwrights to embed social and political arguments within their play's context. In what are often labelled "theatre of fact" or "documentary drama," writers have often used actual events "to explore their culture's growing concern for guilt and responsibility in public affairs and morality" (Brockett 1982, 680).

In Europe in the 1960s, playwrights like Peter Weiss, Martin Walser, and Tankred Dorst wrote politically responsible works. In France in the late 1970s, Jean-Claude Grumbert and André Benedetto were among those who produced socially conscious plays that "drew attention to political and social justice" (Brockett 1982, 681).

The presence of this type of drama rises and wanes over decades. Peter Brook (1965), director and writer, has said that with the need to address public affairs and morality in their work, the problem of playwrights today is this: "how [to] make plays dense in experience" yet still engage the audience (v).

9

Interviews, Personal Accounts, Comments by Playwrights

Tony Kushner's Views on AIDS and Obstacles to Creating and Staging a Script

The first part of Tony Kushner's epic *Angels in America* won the Pulitzer Prize for drama and the Tony Award for best play in 1993. A radical vision of American society, politics, and religion set against the AIDS epidemic and the Reagan years, *Millennium Approaches* was joined in repertory by Part 2, *Perestroika*, on Broadway at the Walter Kerr Theater.

In the following article, the playwright reflects on the influence of friendship and collaboration on the creation of the plays. (Kushner's article appeared in the *New York Times* [21 November 1993]: 1, 30–31.)

IS IT A FICTION THAT PLAYWRIGHTS CREATE ALONE?

"Angels in America," Parts 1 and 2, has taken five years to write, and as the work nears completion I find myself thinking a great deal about the people who have left their traces in these texts. The fiction that artistic labor happens in isolation, and that artistic accomplishment is exclusively the provenance of individual talents, is politically charged, and, in my case at least, repudiated by the facts.

While the primary labor on "Angels" has been mine, more than two dozen people have contributed words, ideas and structures to these plays, including actors, directors, audiences, one-night stands, my former lover and many friends. Two in particular, my closest friend, Kimberly Flynn ("Perestroika" is dedicated to her), and the man who commissioned "Angels," helped shape it and co-directed the Los Angeles production, Oskar Eustis, have had profound influence. Had I written these plays without the participation of my collaborators, they would be entirely different—would, in fact, never have come to be.

Americans pay high prices for maintaining the Myth of the Individual: [W]e have no system of universal health care, we don't educate our children, we can't pass sane gun-control laws, we hate and fear inevitable processes like aging and dying.

Way down, close to the bottom of the list of the evils Individualism visits on our culture is the fact that in the modern era it isn't enough to write; you must also be a Writer and play your part as the protagonist in a cautionary narrative in which you will fail or triumph, be in or out, hot or cold. The rewards can be fantastic; the punishment dismal; it's a zero-sum game, and its guarantor of value, its marker, is that you pretend to play it solo, preserving the myth that you alone are the wellspring of your creativity.

When I started to write these plays I wanted to attempt something of ambition and size even if that meant I might be accused of straying too close to ambition's ugly twin, pretentiousness. Given the bloody opulence of this country's great and terrible history, given its newness and grand improbability, its artists are bound to be tempted toward large gestures and big embraces, a proclivity de Tocqueville deplored as a national artistic trait more than 150 years ago. Melville, my favorite American writer, strikes inflated even hysterical chords on occasion. It's the sound of the individual ballooning, overreaching. We are all children of the "Song of Myself."

Anyone interested in exploring alternatives to Individualism and the political economy it serves, Capitalism, has to be willing to ask hard questions about the ego, both as abstraction and as exemplified in oneself.

Bertolt Brecht, while he was still in Weimar-era Berlin and facing the possibility of participating in a socialist revolution, wrote a series of remarkable short plays, his *Lehrstücke*, or learning-plays. The principal subject of these plays was the painful dismantling, as a revolutionary exigency, of the individual ego. His metaphor for this dismantling is death.

(Brecht, who never tried to hide the dimensions of his own titanic personality, didn't sentimentalize the problems such personalities present, or the process of loss involved in attempting to let go of the richness, and the riches, that accompany such successful self-creation.)

He simultaneously claimed and mocked the identity he'd won for himself, "a great German writer," raising important questions about the means of literary production, challenging the sacrosanctity of the image of the solitary artist and, at the same time, openly, ardently wanting to be recognized as a genius. That he was a genius is inarguably the case. For a man deeply committed to collectivity as an ideal and an achievable political goal, this blazing singularity was a mixed blessing at best and at worst an obstacle to a blending of radical theory and practice.

In the lower-right-hand corner of the title page of many of Brecht's plays you will find, in tiny print, a list of names under the heading "collaborators." Sometimes these people contributed little, sometimes a great deal. One cannot help feeling that those who bore those minuscule names, who expended the considerable labor the diminutive typography conceals, have had a bum deal. Many of these collaborators, Ruth Berlau, Elisabeth Hauptmann, Margarete Steffin, were women. On the question of shared intellectual and artistic labor, gender is always an issue.

On the last day last spring when the Tony nominations were being handed out, I left the clamorous room at Sardi's thinking gloomily that here was another source of anxiety, another obstacle to getting back to work rewriting "Perestroika." In the building's lobby, I was introduced to the producer Elizabeth R. McCann, who said to me: "I've been worried about how you were handling all this till I read that you have an Irish woman in your life." Ms. McCann was referring to Kimberly Flynn. An article in *The New Yorker* last year about "Angels in America" described how certain features of our shared experience dealing with her prolonged health crisis, caused by a serious cab accident several years ago, had a major impact on the plays.

. . . In a wonderful recent collection of essays on creative partnerships, "Significant Others," edited by Isabelle De Courtivron and Whitney Chadwick, the contributors examine both healthy and deeply unhealthy versions of artistic interdependence in such couples as the Delaunays, Kahlo and Rivers, Hammett and Hellman, and Jasper Johns and Robert Rauschenberg—and in doing so strike forcefully at what the editors call "the myth of solitariness."

Since this myth is all important to our view of artistic work, we have no words for the people to whom we are indebted. I call Oskar Eustis a dramaturg, sometimes a collaborator; but collaborator implies co-authorship and nobody knows what dramaturg implies. "Angels" began in a conversation, real and imaginary, with Oskar. A romantic-ambivalent love for American history and belief in what one of the play's characters calls "the prospect of some sort of radical democracy spreading outward and growing up" are things Oskar and I share, part of the discussions we had for nearly a year before I started writing Part 1. Oskar continues to be for me, intellectually and emotionally, what the developmental psychologists call "a secure base of attachment" (a phrase I learned from Kimberly).

The play is indebted, too, to writers I've never met. It's ironical that Harold Bloom, in his introduction to "Musical Variations on Jewish Thought" by Lovier Revault D'Allones, provided me with a translation of the Hebrew word for "blessing"—"more life"—which subsequently became key to the heart of "Perestroika." Professor Bloom is also the author of "The Anxiety of Influence," his oedepilization [*sic*] of the history of western literature, which, when I first encountered it years ago, made me so anxious my analyst suggested I put it away. Recently I had the chance to meet Professor Bloom and, guilty over my appropriation of "more life," I fled from the encounter as one of Freud's "Totem and Taboo" tribesmen might flee from a meeting with that primal father, the one with the big knife. (I cite Professor Bloom as the source of the idea in the published script.)

Guilt, of course, plays a part in this confessional account; and I want the people who helped me make these plays to be identified because their labor was consequential. Many important names have not been mentioned, lest this begin to sound like a thank-you note or, worse, an acceptance speech. I have been blessed with remarkable comrades and collaborators: [T]ogether we organize the world for ourselves, or at least we organize our understanding of it; we reflect it, refract it, criticize it, grieve over its savagery, and help one another to discern, amidst the gathering dark, paths of resistance, pockets of peace and places from whence hope may be plausibly expected.

Marx was right: [T]he smallest indivisible human unit is two people, not one; one is fiction. From such nets of souls, societies, the social world, [and] human life spring. And also plays.

Edward Albee's Comments on Playwriting

Edward Albee holds three Pulitzer Prizes for drama: *A Delicate Balance* in 1967, *Seascape* in 1975, and *Three Tall Women* in 1994. The following are statements by Albee on the theatre's need for well-prepared scripts.

It seems to me that it is the playwright's responsibility to come as close as he can to the ideal—the ideal is that everything that has gone before, the nature of the characters, the style that the play is written in, the author's intention, is so precise that any sentence that comes in the middle of a play can be spoken only in one way and understood only in one way (quoted in Kolin 1988, 33). . . . We've been breeding playwrights who think of themselves only as craftsmen rather than artists, and bad craftsmen at that, who consider themselves small cogs in the wheel. . . . The craft is not imprecise; the relationship between playwright and audience has become enormously imprecise, basically because the playwrights have been abdicating their responsibility to their craft (33).

> On November 29, 1995, Albee's nationally televised address to the National Press Club in Washington D.C. challenged the impediments to production of dramatic scripts in America. Excerpts from the address follow.

I like being a playwright, which is fortunate—(laughter)—since it's one of the few things that I can do with any competence. I like the immediacy of the theater. I like the fact that the theater always exists in the present tense, and that at its best it is an argument against the status quo. A serious play always holds a mirror up to people and says, "Look, this is who you are. This is how you behave. If you don't like it, why don't you change? This is the function of all of the serious arts in the United states, and is one of the serious dilemmas we have in this extraordinary country, the lack of healthy relationship between those who take the trouble to create arts in our society, and those for whom the trouble is taken, for whom the arts are created.

. . . Mind you, I would rather be a writer in the United States than [in] any other country I have visited. The occasional hostility, the occasional indifference, the intentional misunderstanding that creative artists face in a democracy such as the United States is nothing, is child's play compared to the literal life and death matter of daring to speak out as a journalist, as a creative artist, in many, many countries. . . .

So being a writer in the United States is child's play. It is basically nothing. . . . There is nobody in the United States right now to tell us, "no, you may not read that book. No, you may not look at that newspaper. No, you may not harbor that thought. . . . No, you may not participate in the arts as you will." There is nobody to tell us this, with the possible exception of commerce in our society, which in some ways strikes me as being the equivalent of the thought control in dictatorial societies. But aside from commerce in this country, there is nobody to deny us access to all of these tough truths that the arts can tell us except for the one person, ourselves. We deny ourselves so much. We deny ourselves access to those arts which may trouble and disturb us. We are the censors of our selves. It is enormously damaging and enormously dangerous what we do.

. . . The only reason that the arts really matter is that the arts are one of the few things that distinguish us from all the other animals. We invented the arts to define ourselves to ourselves, to define consciousness to ourselves, and we live still in a society where there is nobody to deny us access to the tough truths that the arts can tell us, nobody yet except ourselves.

(Question from the moderator of the program)

Mr. Karmin: What can be done to revive serious theatre in this country? [And] what accounts for the theatre's demise anyway?

Mr. Albee: Theatre has not died. The arts in America have not died. We probably have more good playwrights in the United States now than we have ever had, to my memory. We have more interesting young painters and sculptors and novelists and poets than we've ever had in this country. It is just that it's getting tougher and tougher and tougher for them to reach a mass audience. This is part of the commercial censorship that we have in our society. The people who fill the Broadway theatres with those lugubrious musicals these days—(laughter)—to make the theatre safe for people who do not wish to have a useful experience in the theatre—(laughter)—if they were told that the audience wanted to see Samuel Beckett and Chekhov and Pirandello, the Broadway theatres would be filled with Beckett, Chekhov, and Pirandello. It all comes down to what they believe will sell.

The greatest novels and books of poetry published in the United States are not the best sellers. A number of book stores in the United States act as a kind of censor by not carrying the finest books that are published, but only the mass sellers that they know will move and sell thousands and thousands and thousands of copies. This is a kind of commercial censorship of the arts . . . based solely upon what will sell. It is a crippling form of censorship but is tolerated only by people who wish to tolerate it. If we had a society filled with people who wanted to participate as a natural part of their lives, as natural as breathing in all of the serious arts, if we were able to grow a couple of generations of people who cared about the serious arts, if our educational structure and our educational system permitted this, and if our government was not determined to destroy the aesthetic education of the people in this country, we might conceivably raise a generation of people who would not tolerate the mediocrity of what is being pushed and sold in the arts in this country. We can have it. As I said about democracy before, we can have anything we want. But look around you: We're getting what we deserve.

10

The Playwright's Interaction with the Theatre Team

The ticklish tie between playscript and performance makes the rehearsal process as precarious as it is imperative. Historians note that William Shakespeare, aware of the trials in staging, routinely involved himself in rehearsals. With a "manager's sense of the public" gained from long experience as manager-writer-actor, Shakespeare handled "with practiced and inventive skill all the available resources of his professional medium" (G. B. Evans 1974, 4). Hence "the fundamental certainty about Shakespeare" is that he interacted with his production team—a man of the theatre "to his fingertips" (47).

Today's dramatists, too, have needed time and opportunity to modify and adjust their creation. Indeed, painters, sculptors, composers, and writers in many areas reenvision, revise, and restructure their work from a drive to send their artistic vision to audiences intact. In the early twentieth century, novelist F. Scott Fitzgerald made seventeen complete revisions of his brilliant novel *Tender Is the Night* before he deemed it finished; the number of revisions Fitzgerald's *The Great Gatsby* underwent is not expressly known. With theatre's innate tie between playscript and performance, our writers' urges to shelter their works of art during production may linger even longer than in other creative fields.

If a playwright chooses to involve himself in staging his own script from rehearsal to performance, his interaction with other members of the production team gives him an inside job on the script's journey to viewers. During the years that Alan Schneider directed playwright Edward Albee's dramas, Albee often attended rehearsals, watching Schneider's artistry at work. Schneider is remembered for treating a text as "spring, head, and fountain" of staging.[1] His interaction with his theatre team made rehearsals a time for collaboration. Albee has declared that he learned as much about playwriting as directing by watching Schneider stage *Who's Afraid of Virginia Woolf?, A Delicate Balance,* and other Albee plays in the 1960s–1970s.[2]

Albee's notion seems feasible. At Schneider's rehearsals, Albee listened to lines he had written, observed scenes he had planned, and experienced his script in full dimension. With sound, look, and rhythm crystallized on stage, a clever playwright could test what he had first envisioned for his play against what his written words were now sending to the stage. This chance for a playwright to test a script during rehearsal seems a viable justification for playwrights to involve themselves in production. With today's playwrights, this use of rehearsal time and space for shaping their visions to the actuality of performance is once again, as with Shakespeare, becoming a milestone choice.

In 1992, Edward Albee continued this long-standing tradition of involving himself with his actors and designers during rehearsals. When the University of Houston and the Houston International Festival Committee commissioned him to write a play about Spain, he wrote *The Lorca Play: Scenes from a Life* and chose to direct it himself. His wish to be along on the job could curb the sometime conflicts of playwrights and directors. Close collaboration with his designers, actors, and stage crew in production would shape the script to the stage.

EDWARD ALBEE'S REHEARSAL PROCESS FOR *THE LORCA PLAY* (1992)

Rehearsals for Edward Albee's *The Lorca Play* (1992) held immediate and ongoing challenges for its theatre team. Because of the play's unique nature, smooth collaboration among the members of the team would be crucial. Unlike many of Albee's previous works, *The Lorca Play* had a pageantlike form and a cast of thirty-seven. As Albee, with his set, sound, and light designers and a mix of Equity and student actors, tackled the play's complex form, their interaction turned the script's visions into actualities on stage.

The Lorca Play addresses specific issues of artistic freedom through its focus on the atrocities that ended the career of playwright Federico Garcia Lorca in 1936. Lorca, Spain's great Romantic author, was assassinated by government and church authorities in Spain's revolution-torn 1920s and 1930s. The play weighs the censorship of writers in Spain and, by extension, those in the world at large; it focuses on a wide slice of society—artists, musicians, Spanish townspeople, and heads of Church and State. The content encompasses world events, among them Spain's revolution and the birth of its second Republic, America's great depression and the collapse of Wall Street. Albee and his team used rehearsals to confront the conflicts *The Lorca Play* presented. The reach of the play's action would generate projection problems. Viewers would need help to surmount time-and-space hurdles if they were to follow Lorca from the old world to the new, from youth to premature death. Initially, Albee had envisioned three actors to depict the Spanish writer at different ages. Yet even before rehearsals, he had simplified his concept to two rather than three actors: Young Lorca (Robert Martin) and Lorca-as-Adult (Wade Mylius). As the play developed on stage, director Albee and designer John Gow worked together to test light and shadow, making them serve as innuendo to lift the two Lorcas over the script's conceptual walls of past and present, of there and here. Light would transfer the Adult or the Young Lorca (and us) from one group to another, from one decade to the next. Because Albee wanted us to see the child-side of the adult, both Lorca-actors might need to appear simultaneously. The two could stand left or right of curtain yet through skillfully placed spots be visible, even speak to us while we concentrated upon other lighted figures center stage. Our eyes switched to frantic New York crowds in the late 1920s where we watched the crash of Wall Street, or to Cuba where we saw Lorca's work with theatre groups. We passed easily through the years in which Franco and the Cardinal had inveighed against Lorca's artistic freedom, taken his life, and for decades thereafter, buried his literary legacy.

From the start of rehearsal, as the director-playwright worked with his actors and designers, they promptly updated the script's sheets to record each ongoing decision on content or staging. The revisions affected, to varying degrees, the setting, focus, dialogue, and style of delivery. The shifts in the script's setting were both conceptual and functional. Although Albee's scripted vision for the play's backdrop (a view of Granada) had been set from the start and remained so throughout rehearsals, his concept was less fixed for stairs and platforms on which the play's narrator (Michael Marich) and other principals would take their places and deliver lines. On the rehearsal stage, noting the stage picture, Albee and his team could test options for positioning the actor playing Lorca (Wade Mylius) among the cast's other principals. Throughout the play, Albee needed Lorca mobile. At times he must appear with an ensemble of actors portraying Lorca's contemporaries. He must also appear in family groups, and at times with his enemies—the heads of Spanish Church and State (the Catholic Cardinal and Generalissimo Franco) who opposed his writings as heretical threats to their status. As rehearsals progressed, Albee and scenic designer Arch Andrus worked out details for three stage levels: the stage floor for Lorca's interaction with family and friends; a middle level with small platforms for the narrator and other principals; and a third level for his enemies—a catwalk extending across the stage. On this catwalk, the actors playing the major instigators in the censorship of Lorca would appear: Generalissimo Franco (Peter Baquet) and his aide-de-camp (Jason Douglas) would sit or stand left stage, and on the other side, the Catholic Cardinal (James Belcher, Equity actor) and his priest (Wade Hescht).

Albee's presence at rehearsals allowed trial-and-error decisions on stage properties. What the team saw and heard on stage might suggest the wisdom of less sound or motion. In one scene, a wagon was brought on stage with two actresses on board.[3] The script called for them to recite passages from popular Lorca plays, backed up by a flamenco guitarist (Tom McCall). After confronting the stage picture, however, Albee and his sound designers realized that continuous music could distract an audience from the Lorca readings; thereafter the guitarist played only a few measures at the start and at the finish of the recitation.

These rehearsal adjustments to setting and props occurred more immediately than those involving style of presentation. At early rehearsals, actors had delivered vital monologues and lines of exposition in a confrontational mode. Albee's constant involvement with his actors helped him reenvision the scenes with a less stark presentation. The early script had called for the narrator (Michael Marich) to speak directly to the audience—"out, in a narrative tone"—as he filled in the play's exposition.[4] Working with Marich, Albee sought more interaction between the narrator and the other actors on stage; they gradually framed gestures or retorts between the narrator and characters on the stage floor below him. As the narrator addressed the audience, he might lean from his midlevel platform to look for a moment directly at Lorca or at those near him on stage level, eliciting from them either a few words or a riveting reaction. These contacts soon gave the feel of actual communication rather than straight exposition, softening the effect and bringing the audience into the scene.

This emphasis on involving the audience in stage pictures also turned the narrator's stiff, conventional introductions of characters to the audience into good theatre. The initial, decorous formality had lagged with its vital details on each principal's place in Spanish history. Noting the effect, Albee and the narrator opted to reduce the stasis by injecting stage business between those introduced and others on stage. When the narrator brought elderly Spanish composer Manuel DeFalla (Paul Prince) to the stage, Albee achieved a moving stage picture by sending the maid (Marisa Castaneda) to help DeFalla ascend the steps to the platform where he would sit throughout the introductions. Graciously, DeFalla turned to her to say, "Thank you," and the maid, smiling, added, "You're welcome."[5]

Rehearsals also offered Albee and his actors time and opportunity to discuss their roles and a credible embodiment of them on stage. For a pivotal scene in which Lorca (Wade Mylius) must recite an expressionistic poem—"I Want to Sleep the Dream of Apples," Mylius experimented with tone, stance, and rhythm. He tried the recitation from a kneeling position, then from a semiupright stance, each with variations in body language. Ultimately, both actor and author-director opted for Lorca to stand rather than kneel obtrusively.

An obvious benefit gained by Albee's interaction with his team was the ease with which he could shift or intensify his authorial focus. Increasingly he emphasized Young Lorca's presence in Adult Lorca's spirit, perhaps to help viewers see Lorca's nature as simple and unassuming rather than wildly radical, as his enemies were claiming. For Act I, Scene iii, the decision to focus more strongly on Young Lorca brought freshness and directness. In the early version, the narrator's opening monologue had supplied only general matter on Adult Lorca, on his country's long-delayed acceptance of him as a writer. As the play came to life in rehearsals, Albee and his narrator worked on how to help prospective viewers identify with Lorca more intimately so that they would want to involve themselves with his tragedy. Hence the narrator delivered more introspective comments on Lorca's lingering ties to his youth. From his midlevel platform, the narrator, concentrating on Young Lorca on the first level below, explained to viewers, "The young Lorca stays with us of course [during the rest of the play]. . . . Doesn't our young self always stay with us—lurk around the edges of our consciousness?"[6] Published letters of Federico Garcia Lorca after his death attest to his twofold nature: "In the depths of my being there is a powerful desire to be a little child, very humble and very retiring" (Gibson 1989, 74). In subsequent blocking, Albee kept the boy ever closer to Lorca to bridge for viewers the surreal separation between the maturing artist and his boyhood.

With this harmonious collaboration on stage pictures, Adult Lorca could now reach out to touch his "self-as-child" whenever Lorca, sensing the dark in his future, sought to feel safe by connecting to his past. This new blocking directed the adult to lean toward the boy and call out to him, "Never leave me; never go away; never let me lose sight of you."[7] Audiences would be aware that the "child" was still embedded in the "self" of Lorca.

At other spots, the smooth rehearsal process added more focus on the love between Lorca and his mother. In an episode with the artist so distraught that he warns his family, "I have to get away!" the mother's pain and her gestures of fear would increase viewers' awareness of the bond between mother and son. Elsewhere, too, the focus grew stronger on Young Lorca and his mother by letting her reach out to soothe the boy whenever she perceived that the adult, driven from her by approaching political guile, needed her sustenance.[8] These touches would show viewers a Lorca who was not the outcast pervert despised by Church and State but a sensitive, caring human whom family and friends prized.

Touchy points in Lorca's spirituality became clear through smooth rehearsal interaction. The team trimmed nonessential components from an episode with Young and Adult Lorca playfully recalling Lorca's childhood attendance at Mass. In the scene as first rehearsed, Young Lorca had accepted assorted shawls and capes from the watching ensemble and donned them "childishly and dramatically"; he had pranced about, "gesturing in an exaggerated manner, imitating a priest at mass"[9] as the ensemble awkwardly repeated the words of the Mass after him. At this point, the touchy Cardinal, watching from the top level, would yell "Blasphemy!" at the childish playing on the stage floor below him. Albee, with his innate disdain for "spectacle," decided to reblock the scene less sensationally; in the ultimate staging, the boy neither dons the robes, nor prances about; Young and Adult Lorca together recite the words of the Mass with dignity and less exaggeration—though the hard-nosed Cardinal's blast of "Blasphemy!" still issues from his catwalk. This recast scene renders the Cardinal's violent reaction less lucid than ludicrous. It will also foreshadow for future viewers the approach of more violent stabs at Lorca from Church and State.

Of especial help to the playwright-as-director was the rehearsal opportunity to test his plan for actors to recite selections from the historical Lorca's poetry—often monologues in effect. Albee, hearing the student-actors deliver the material, was pleased with their talent yet concerned that the number of readings he had planned from Lorca's works might be gratuitous. During rehearsals, he determined that the number could be reduced without losing the flavor of Lorca's rich romanticism. In Act I, Scene iii, Albee cut three Lorca poems entirely (including the highly acclaimed "King of Harlem") and kept only six of eleven verses of "The Poem of the Deep South" for recitation.[10] Those he retained were seemly, focusing on impending gloom or death by violence; they would prepare the audience for the fate approaching Lorca from the State's total restriction of his artistic freedom. During the collaborative polishing of the play, Albee also listened to each word and phrase he had given Lorca-actor Mylius, anticipating the force they would have on viewers. When dissatisfied, he sought an even stronger effect so that audiences would perceive the character's sensitivity and expressionistic flair. In an episode with the Cardinal threatening to excommunicate Lorca for his non-Christian notions of Christ and for his lack of fealty to the Spanish State, Albee now inserted for Lorca-actor Mylius a plea to viewers to understand artists and their "special and dangerous talent."[11] With rehearsal testing of his delivery, the actor faces the audience beyond the footlights to ask, "Do you know what it's like to be completely misunderstood . . .

to fall in love with people who don't want you? Do you know what it is like to be me?"[12] At the premiere, the hush that followed the plea showed the caliber of the insertion.

For the play's grim finale, the scene shop designers put extra force into Lorca's last hours as his family and friends furtively watched his execution. The crew constructed a huge canvas facsimile of Goya's *Executions of the Third of May* (1814) as backdrop for the final moments. Goya's painting shows a group of Madrilenos facing a firing squad. With the advantage of rehearsal testing, the crew could determine precisely how and when the canvas should drop for the sharpest audience impact. To show Lorca's mettle, Albee inserted new dialogue into the play's crisp, minimalist execution scene. In his last moments, Lorca flings a terse protest at his Falangist executioner (John Livingstone): "You mustn't do this—this isn't fair"—a denouncement that incites the bully-killer to retort sardonically, "Oh No?" and then scream at his men, "Ready, Aim, Fire!"[13] Art critics have written that the young man in Goya's canvas flung up his arms to defy the soldiers (Canaday 1988, 290). He, like Lorca, might have called out, "You mustn't do this! This isn't fair!"

Albee's vision from the start had been to create on stage a mirror of the Goya masterpiece. He was also familiar with folklore accounts still-circulating today, eyewitness claims in oral literature that Lorca, after the first volley of bullets, had pulled himself to his knees to scream "Look, I'm still alive" before a second round felled him. Through exacting rehearsal trials, Albee and his theatre team supplied a consummate stage moment for prospective audiences. After the last burst of guns, Young Lorca, ready to exit left stage with his family, looks back and sees the body of Lorca move. Instantly the boy turns from the exit, edges toward the body, and reaches out as if to touch the dying Lorca. But the boy pauses, backs away, and rushes offstage, screaming for his departing mother and father.[14] With this added stage business, the theatre team pulls us one final time toward the child in Lorca who, like the adult, had justly expected to live out a normal life span.

These "Scenes from a Life" in *The Lorca Play* heap philosophical weight upon Lorca's protest against all Church or State proscription of dissenters. The staging says to the audience, "This isn't fair!" The theatre team's exemplary collaboration has made it possible to shock the audiences into awareness of the hazards of repression of artistic freedom. For future Lorca audiences, the playwright-director's presence at rehearsals had been opportune—a time to cherish. His chance to work with his theatre team translated his scripted vision of repression into "a poetry of the theatre" (Copeau 1913, quoted in Brockett 1982, 578). Who wouldn't identify with a playwright's wish to be along on the job?

Albee's Role as Social Critic

After the premiere performance of Edward Albee's *The Lorca Play: Scenes from a Life* (1992), an article entitled "An Elegy for Thwarted Vision" appeared in the *Journal of Dramatic Theory and Criticism* (Luere 1995, 142–47). It praised Albee as a social critic indicting political injustice. A *JDTC* stance has been that one value of playwrights to society lies in their focus on ironic overlaps between other countries' cultural mores and our own. Excerpts from the article appear here with permission of *JDTC*'s editors, John Gronbeck Tedesco and Kent Neely.

AN ELEGY FOR THWARTED VISION

For over three decades, Edward Albee's controversial dramas have kept him in the critical and public consciousness. With self-assurance, Albee has disregarded commercial pressure, experimenting with dramatic form and thrusting innovative theatre at his audiences.[1] How natural, now, to find Albee evolving a play on the need for artistic freedom. His 1992 venture, *The Lorca Play: Scenes from a Life*, is more than a political or social tract; it is an elegy for any artist's thwarted vision.

The play's protagonist, Federico Garcia Lorca (c. 1900–1936), was the Spanish poet-playwright executed during the Fascist reign of General Francisco Franco. In two acts, ten scenes, and a pageant-like structure, Albee takes us inside the soul of a casualty. Still in progress after its 1992 premiere, the play dramatizes Albee's views on the thwarting of Lorca's literary vision by State and Church throughout Franco's forty-year reign. Lorca had written his "unorthodox poetry and plays when censorship momentarily lessened with the birth of Spain's short-lived Second Republic (proclaimed in 1931) (Brockett 1982, 612). Without being an agit-prop [*sic*] piece, *The Lorca Play* is in part a polemic on the plight of artists in a culture that restricts and censors their work. . . .

Rather than belabor us with didactic monologues on repression, Albee uses parody to approach the parallels between Lorca's culture and our own (E. Evans 1992, sec. D, p. 3). With Franco on stage in military uniform and the Cardinal in formal vestment, Albee's script quips, "Don't lose sight of *them*. . . . It's people like that who run the world—people who define our faith, who give us our identity."[2] Albee's lines alert us that "they" could be anywhere: "Sometimes they don't wear those uniforms; sometimes a suit and tie does them just fine; sometimes a suit and tie does them even better."[3] Houston critics picked up on the parallels: One wrote that Franco's denunciation of Lorca's work "could have been lifted from a stump speech damning the N.E.A.'s funding of obscene and outside-the-mainstream art" (Albright 1992, sec D., p. 2); another critic echoed him, recalling "America's current art wars" in which writers had to "fend off attacks" on their artistic content" (E. Evans 1992, sec. D, p. 3). Albee's action shows both Franco and the Catholic Cardinal harassing Lorca: Franco loathes his writing for its jabs at totalitarian rule, and the Cardinal threatens to excommunicate him for non-standard religious concepts.[4] . . .

To acquaint us with the culture that shaped Lorca as person and artist, Albee's scenes reach toward the land and people of Spain, "the country which birthed him . . . and the country which killed him."[5] We move on undismayed through the years in which Franco and the Cardinal had inveighed against Lorca's artistic freedom, taken away his life, and for decades thereafter, hidden his literary legacy. Albee uses a narrator in droll scenes to mock the bogus ethics of the self-righteous clergy. When Act II begins, with Cardinal and Priest missing from their places near Franco and his aide, the narrator looks off-stage-right and barks, "Would you two get out here, please?"[6] Franco, too, glances off-right to ask, "What ARE they doing," and his Aide suggests, "I think it's what they might have BEEN doing."[7] When the upbraided two slip in and begin to mount the stairs, we see the Cardinal "buttoning the front of *his* gown, followed by the Priest, pulling down the back of his own—and we hear the Cardinal mutter, "All right! For heaven's sake."[8] Although Albee tastefully keeps all other scenes between Cardinal and Priest (and between Lorca and his alleged intimates) tightly restrained rather than emotionally flamboyant, here he lets us smile very mildly at the hypocrisy of the Church's ban on diversity.

To deride the State's brutal drive for conformity, Albee gives Franco and his aide street-and-gutter-level language. When Franco offers asinine excuses for eliminating dissenters, Albee lets him brag coarsely that after he had "saved the country from itself," there were "some people just didn't make the cut, if you catch my drift . . . weren't worth talking about anymore."[9] . . . When the narrator objects, "Oh, I see . . . so Lorca's name vanished, eh? . . . his poems taken out of print," Franco replies, "Yeah, like that. He wasn't worth the trouble. . . . Who cares? Commie faggot!"[10]

It was Lorca's theater work that deviated most pointedly from the State's main-line precepts. In his *Lorca Play*, Albee has an actor refer to a news report that charged Lorca with "perverting the peasants" through staged displays "of shameful promiscuity . . . of free love," and with "obedience to the dictates of Jewish Marxism, free love, and communism."[11] Albee's Franco explicitly names the actors "atheists" and "homosexuals."[12] Historically, Lorca had become active in the group to revive the "rancid and stagnant" Spanish theater from its "dead reproductions of the classics and escapist junk"; he preferred "theater *for* the people, *about* them."[13] His insistence that theater "should immerse itself in the problems assailing humanity" (Gibson 1989, 431) suggests Albee's own drive for fresh and useful theater in the early 1960s. (Roudané, in Bloom 1987, 163). From start to finish, Albee's through-line for *The Lorca Play* is that Lorca's haunting, idealistic vision for theater was political poison for him in a Fascist country that subordinated the individual (creative artist or not) to the combined will of Church and State.

Mocking the inescapable outcome of Church-and-State collusion, Albee gives us amusing scenes with the Cardinal toadying to the overbearing egoism of Franco. Albee's dialogue let Franco boast to the Cardinal, "My mother was a saint!" to which the Cardinal mumbles only, "She was?"[14] But Franco quickly insists, "You don't think my mother was a saint?"— to which the fawning Cardinal replies, "I do, I do. . . . If you say she was a saint, she was a saint!"[15] At another spot, Albee ridicules the Church's subservience to the State by forcing Franco to overhear the narrator's jest, "There's talk of making Isabella a Saint. . . . Shows you what a few good works can do!"[16] (In Spain's early years, Isabella is said to have ordered her country's gypsies, Jews, and Arabs, "Convert or be killed!"[17])

Through this requiem on the thwarting of Lorca's vision by political pressures, Albee dramatizes Spain's tragic loss: a lifetime of productivity from a literary giant. Its shocking scenes confirm Albee's grasp of art and history, and heap philosophical weight onto artists' protests against the narrowness of political and social repression—"This isn't fair." Albee's *The Lorca Play* shows the playwright fulfilling his own role as a social critic.

NOTES

1. *Macbeth*, Act II, Sc. iii, 1.

2. Edward Albee, Preface to Alan Schneider's *Entrances* (New York: Viking Penguin, 1986). See also Terrence McNally, "Edward Albee in Conversation," in Philip C. Kolin, ed., *Conversations with Edward Albee* (Jackson and London: University of Mississippi Press, 1988), 199. Also, Dramatist-Director Forum at Annual Inge Festival, Independence, Kansas, April 1989.

Edward Albee's Rehearsal Process for *The Lorca Play* (1992)

The Lorca Play: Form A denotes the script at the outset of March 1992 rehearsals, Form B to the script after the rehearsal process, the one followed for the production in April-May 1992.

3. *The Lorca Play*, Act II, Sc. ii [Form A:1; Form B:1].
4. Act II, Sc. i [Form A:7; Form B:6].
5. Act I, Sc. i [Form B:9].
6. Act I, Sc. iii [Form A:14–15; B:11].
7. Act I, Sc. ii [Form A:10; Form B:8].
8. Act II, Sc. i [Form B:8].

9. Act I, Sc. ii [Form A:13; Form B:10].
10. Act I, Sc. iii [Form A:3–13; B:1–4].
11. Act I, Sc. v [Form B:4].
12. Ibid.
13. Act II, Sc. v [Form A:2; Form B:2].
14. Ibid.

Albee's Role as Social Critic

1. Matthew Roudané's comments on America's "theatrical renaissance" in Harold Bloom, ed., *Modern Critical Views: Edward Albee* (New York: Chelsea House Publishers, 1987), 163.
2. *The Lorca Play*, Act I, Sc. i, p. 5.
3. Ibid.
4. Act I, Sc. ii, p. 11.
5. Act II, Sc. i, p. 6.
6. Ibid., pp. 3–4.
7. Ibid., p. 4.
8. Ibid., p. 7.
9. Ibid.
10. Ibid.
11. Act II, Sc. ii, p. 1.
12. Ibid.
13. Ibid.
14. Act I, Sc. ii, p. 11.
15. Ibid.
16. Ibid., p. 3.
17. Ibid.

PART IV
THE DESIGNER

11

The Designer's Role

DESIGNERS' MOVEMENT OF AUTHORS' INTENT TO STAGE AND AUDIENCE

The elements of design carry a playwright's vision to viewers and, in associative fashion, make both subtle and strong statements about the playwright's intent. Elements of design like light, pattern, shape, and sound strike audiences early, pulling them into participation in the play. Design helps viewers catch the playwright's intentions for mood, style, and intensity. Early in production, the designers must determine what the stage design will say to those beyond the footlights.

Deliberate use of design, whether realistic, abstract, or symbolic, can give the author's script a dramatic thrust (Cohen 1983, 97). When we read Aristotle's classic references to the "spectacle of theatre," a phrase referring to the impact of the stage on our vision, the words still bring to our minds the art of designers as well as the talent of playwright, director, and actor. A director's dialogue with designers must be open and ongoing to move the script's ambience, tone, and image to viewers. Whether a play is to be produced "in the style of the period in which it was written, in the period it was written about, or in modern dress," many facets of design are interrelated (Loney 1990, 101). The style of the costuming, the shape of the stage, type of decor, patterns of movement, intensity of light and sound—each facet is handled by artists in that area. The costume designer can give the actors an appearance that helps us tie them to the scripted characters they portray. The set designer can use scenery and stage pieces (flats, doors, furniture, draperies, windows) as more than just a background for the playwright's scripted action. Special effects themselves have a dynamic role in furthering the playwright's intent. For example, the huge door from which white steam pours onto stage in Arthur Kopit's *Road to Nirvana* heightens the mystery of what weird surgery is being performed on the character who has just passed beyond the door. In Edward Albee's *Box*, the large cube, covered with glo-paint, is centered on the stage floor to focus viewers on a disembodied voice's complaints that our culture's arts are being crowded out by our crafts.

Though an old principle of drama pleads that staging should omit what doesn't add to the play, let us pause before leaving out the creative touches of designers. Their work helps staging meet, nay, surpass an author's expectations. The result—whether spectacle or not—can draw popular and critical interest to the playscript.

12

Interviews, Personal Accounts, Comments by Designers

Claremarie Verheyen, Costume Designer

Claremarie Verheyen discusses theoretical and practical issues in costume design. Designer Verheyen is a member of the faculty of the
University of Houston's School of Theatre.

Question: Through a script's dialogue, stage directions, or action, how
much does a playwright tell the designer about the appearance sets and
costumes should have? Does the playwright include in the script a complete description of design and costumes?

Clairemarie Verheyen: Typically, no. In the script, playwrights tell a story
to some purpose. They want to convey an issue, a moral, an excitement,
or theatricality. Your job as designer is to read the play carefully to learn
what the story is about, and then, through design, to help the audience
understand the author's purpose in telling it. Typically, the playwright's
script gives you numerous clues.

Question: What kind of clues?

Clairemarie Verheyen: It can be clues on how people speak. Their language might be poetic, elevated, or very rhythmic—as Shakespeare's dialogue might be. It might be rough or staccato. You can actually hear,
through the written dialogue, how his characters speak. Then, from *how*
they talk (not merely from what they say), you try to imagine what their
function is—*why* the playwright has written them. You find their func-

tion, too, in how other people talk about them. These clues reveal essential information.

Sometimes, the designer's vision of where to situate the play's action is predicated upon the story itself. Perhaps it could happen only in upstate New York, or on the lower East Side, or on the steps of the New York City library. That information has been given to you by the playwright. With Shakespeare, whose stories are more broadly based than others, the story is so true and profound that it could live in many different environments. With such scripts, you have more flexibility in selection of locale. Other stories, more delicate or more sensitive to their surroundings, will not survive modifications or shifts in environment. Your job as a designer is to discover what the playwright envisioned, then to help the audience understand that. Often, the play's director will have worked out some of this background for you; he may come to you with an interpretation, something he feels the playwright envisioned. Your job then is not necessarily to serve the playwright, but to serve the director.

Question: Might the director have talked with the playwright initially?

Clairemarie Verheyen: In some instances the director and the playwright are good friends, or the director and the playwright have worked together often and have a profound understanding. There are certain directors whom playwrights really love—and directors whom playwrights want to work with because they have more integrity to the written word. Other directors may want to use the written word to launch their own ideas. One director who comes to mind is Robert Wilson, for whom the script itself is not rigidly binding. Wilson is interested in giving the audience some sort of experience that is separate from the script. I find this attitude interesting; I don't know what a playwright would think. I find some adaptations by Robert Wilson interesting. Yet I was appalled at his production of *Danton's Death*, which I had studied in college and had reread before I attended Wilson's rendition of it. It was so distracting that I could not hear the text. With Wilson's *Danton's Death*, the designers had served the director rather than the playwright.

I don't always disagree with that arrangement; it depends on the contractual arrangement and the issues involved. Of course, the director, who has been hired by the theatre, has already contracted to stage his interpretation of that script, and the theatre has obviously agreed. You, as a designer, are working for the theatre, which has agreed to that arrangement. What you must manage, then, is to keep your priorities straight. You are not working for the playwright, nor are you trying solely to illuminate the playwright's vision. Rather, you are trying to illuminate the director's vision since the theatre, by hiring that director, has agreed to it.

Question: Some years ago, what were the arrangements for "vision" and interpretation when you designed the play *Moon for the Misbegotten* here at the School of Theatre?

Clairemarie Verheyen: With *Moon for the Misbegotten*, the ideas we were following came from the play's director, Dr. [Sidney] Berger [Director of the School of Theatre], who had read the play and thought its action and aura fit his concepts of Appalachia, of the region's people, and of their music. Our job as designers was to facilitate, to illuminate, the director's vision.

Question: You had some idea, then, from the director, of what time period to adhere to.

Clairemarie Verheyen: We were trying to depict less a time period than an environment—that of Appalachia. With the costuming, however, we were definitely not striving for honest, realistic Appalachian rag clothes. They would have been boiled repeatedly and passed on from mother to daughter; the material would have been very tired. Since the material of the plot itself was more mythological than realistic, we took liberties with our costumes, making them much brighter and happier than Appalachian clothing might have been.

Question: How realistic was the design for last year's production of Tennessee Williams's *A Streetcar Named Desire* at Houston's regional theatre, The Alley?

Clairemarie Verheyen: I attended the play—though I was not involved in any of its designing.

Question: The dressing of the sisters, Blanche and of Stella, was singularly important since the two were diverse in nature?

Clairemarie Verheyen: Right. Stella is fascinating; she is middle ground, a blending of the "yin and the yang." I think the problem with Blanche is that she is an archetype—pure female. Stanley is an archetype in that he is pure male. Stella is a survivor because, though she is definitely a woman, she is not absolutely 100 percent either—she is the balance. She is much more functional than Blanche, whose needs are superficially female with sensuous, beautiful, feminine clothing, for example. Stella's femininity is more animal—she is the woman's prerogative of recreation.

Question: As a designer, you would have shown that facet of her in her clothes?

Clairemarie Verheyen: Yes. She is a definite design problem when she comes to Stella and Stanley. We know from the script that she is supposed to look like a schoolteacher of the 1950s; we know where she has been, and how she has come to her sister's home. The costumer must put these pieces of information together to grasp what the playwright is insinuating from this "offstage" life.

Question: What if you had been the designer, and the director had told you he wanted her to appear in suggestive, sensuous clothing that you considered inappropriate for the early 1950s? Would you have had the courage to argue with him?

Clairemarie Verheyen: Would I? Of course, I would. Any designer's job would be to approach the director and point out the clues in the story that affect your clothing of her in the performance. Now, the director could say to you as the designer, "I don't care; I want Blanche to look like a street hooker, to look like a slut, to look like someone down on her luck and insane." Your job, if you continue to accept this contract, would then be to show the director the effect of his choice . . . perhaps in a sketch or photograph, so that he could see how his idea would appear on stage to an audience. However, you would also continue to show how you believe Blanche *should* look—e.g., like a traveling, sensuous, very womanly schoolteacher who is trying desperately to keep her life together despite the fact that she is a mess.

Question: What about Stanley?

Clairemarie Verheyen: When he comes in the door saying he has been working on his car, did you believe it for one instant—for one iota of a second? When he says he's been out crawling around under the car, did you buy that? Have you ever seen a fellow after he's come out from under a car?

Question: Yes. He's dirty!

Clairemarie Verheyen: Uh-huh. And his hair wouldn't be quite right, and there'd be a little oil on the face and the hands.

Question: And you, as a designer, would have known that, would you not?

Clairemarie Verheyen: Of course. What also made me wild in that staging was its abuse of all those lines about Blanche in the bathtub—soaking for hours and then emerging from the bath. Have you ever been in a hot bathtub in New Orleans and stepped out of it? How would your hair look?

Question: Stringy?

Clairemarie Verheyen: Oh please! At best, stringy. Yet she keeps saying, "I've just washed my hair." Hello! When she comes out of the bathroom, it's New Orleans, it's summer, it's a sauna; yet she is all wrapped up in a hot thing and her hair is perfect. You don't think that's a problem?

Question: But that designer didn't?

Clairemarie Verheyen: Obviously not. But what we want to know is why nobody noticed these points. Why is Stanley—harried and concerned about his wife—wearing perfectly pressed, knife-pressed, '50s rayon-pleated trousers. Where did he get them, and where was the ironing board?

Question: The designer hadn't read carefully enough to envision these clues?

Clairemarie Verheyen: I wanted to see what pants in New Orleans look like. They don't wear rayon pants in New Orleans because rayon wrinkles so horribly; Stanley would have worn cotton or even linen trousers. Since he's a traveling salesman, he must do something on the road, and he is often gone. He would have had easy-care clothing that allowed him to be on the road. I didn't see any of that either. It was all very confusing. I think the audience became very confused about who Stanley was because his clothing was confusing.

Question: In your costuming of Beckett's *Happy Days* a few years ago, directed by Edward Albee at the Alley, you did well with the pants that Willie (James Belcher) wore. That is, except for the hole from a rip in a seam. (Laughter) Had the script designated what he should wear?

Clairemarie Verheyen: No. Willie does not appear on stage at all until he comes round the mound of sand on stage to crawl toward Winnie. The dialogue tells us that Winnie (Patricia Kilgarriff) remembers him as he was on their wedding day. I asked the director, "Are we seeing him from her point of view?" The answer was "Yes." So, Willie is wearing formal cutaway and striped trousers.

Question: You also contrived Willie's prominent mustache. Is that normally a part of the designer's job?

Clairemarie Verheyen: The designer must create the look of the performer on stage, and part of the look includes facial hair, accessories and hair. In a professional theatre, they might bring in a makeup designer. For our School of Theatre staging, the facial hair was my responsibility. I showed Director Albee different styles of mustache.

Question: You had to know what style came from what period?

Clairemarie Verheyen: My job as designer would be to find out. I would be able to find out from research. A designer would research and investigate options and then give the director some ideas for mustaches from different periods, saying, "This is what mustaches looked like when Winnie was a girl. This is the kind of mustache her husband might have had in that period." If the designer could not have constructed the chosen mustache, someone would have been hired to do it. For our production, Director Albee and I talked initially about a handlebar mustache. He said he wanted it to be made from human hair. I felt that we would not really have the technology nor the time here to construct such a handlebar mustache.

Question: "Here" being an academic theatre.

Clairemarie Verheyen: Right, and a very good one! What I said to the director, however, was that I thought I could build the mustache out of crepe hair or some other material that would be indistinguishable to him or to the audience. After we had discussed the issue, we decided at least to try it; if it didn't work, then we would find another solution. So the first thing we did was to go out and buy some ventilated, hand-tied, handlebar mustaches made of human hair. We had James Belcher, the actor playing this role, wear them; but Mr. Albee did not like them. He described again what he had in mind. What he had wanted was a walrus mustache, not a handlebar mustache. I had misunderstood Mr. Albee's intentions. When they were clarified, I said, "Well, I think I can do that too, so let me try again. We then made, out of wool crepe hair on a latex mold, a mustache—a walrus mustache; we blended it and we put it on James, and triumph! Mr. Albee approved. It was Happy Days. He was happy, and we were happy, and the audience was happy too.

Question: I remember; it was remarkably effective.

Clairemarie Verheyen: Yes. We made enough for the run, enough so that we would have one for each performance.

Question: You needed that many? They don't hold up?

Clairemarie Verheyen: One could have lasted for a couple performances; but they start to flatten out and don't look very good. For a walrus mustache, we wanted to get that twisty bushiness. It ultimately worked very well.

Question: I'll say! A real stage picture! What about Winnie's hair? Do designers customarily do the styling?

Clairemarie Verheyen: Yes. But here the actress actually did her own hair. We were fortunate to have an actress (Patricia Kilgarriff) who had that unique facility and wanted to do it herself. We had offered other choices, telling her we would provide her with somebody to help her with her makeup or her hair. But Winnie wears a hat, puts it on and off. We needed to fit the hat so that it was comfortable. But when the actress said she would do her own hair, we accepted the offer, and the director was very happy with her choice.

Question: How did you know about the style of her hat? Did it say in the script "sunbonnet"?

Clairemarie Verheyen: No, it did not. She was most concerned that the hat be comfortable since she had to sit almost motionless with her head in various strained positions for most of the play. She did not want to worry about the position of the hat. Director Albee had a few suggestions about what kind of hat he wanted. We collected hats of various styles and presented them to her; she put them on, and the director looked at them. We had seen the hats that had been worn in the Broadway production. We also looked at a photograph of the original production directed for Beckett by Alan Schneider.

Question: Was it a large organdy hat?

Clairemarie Verheyen: It was actually more of a picture-book style; Director Albee wanted something that framed her face and that sat comfortably on her head; he wanted something that was also colorful. Though the text says only that she wears a hat, we were relatively flexible in terms of what it was; however, Mr. Albee had a vision of how he wanted it to look; the actress, too, was very specific about its fit.

Question: So you, the designer, needed to help them resolve the hat issue.

Clairemarie Verheyen: Right. It needed to be something that made the director happy and the actress happy.

Question: What about that pesky parasol that appears in almost every scene?

Clairemarie Verheyen: The parasol was fortunately not a costume problem. It became an issue because it had to be a trick parasol, one that explodes. And so Props agreed to take care of that.

Question: It wasn't actually a "costume"—it was a prop?

Clairemarie Verheyen: Ah—a sticky point. That decision is something that has to be agreed upon in early production meetings, to clarify who is doing what. In our process, at the very beginning, we list everything that is needed for the staging. Actually, the Costumes Section took care of many objects for Winnie: She had a hand mirror, a compact, and a brush that we provided because we had them on hand and the director liked them. Parasols often belong to the Costumes Section because they must match the gowns. Since the function of this one was to explode more than to match a dress design, the props department volunteered to acquire and rig this element.

Question: Now I want to ask if design is affected by the type of stage on which the play is produced—whether proscenium, thrust, or arena.

Clairemarie Verheyen: It depends. Certain issues, concerns, or problems are the same on a proscenium stage as on a thrust or in a box or in the round. Naturally, in a theatre-in-the-round, we are very concerned about how the back of the costume looks. On a proscenium stage, viewers certainly see the back at some point; the designer can't totally ignore it. Yet it's certainly not such an issue as on arena or theatre-in-the-round stages, where the backs must be as interesting as the fronts.

Question: On any stage, is care taken to keep the actress who plays the lead in a focal position by giving thought to color or style of costume?

Clairemarie Verheyen: Absolutely. The audience must always be able to find the person who is speaking.

Question: With Williams's Stella and Blanche, did focus fall on either Stella or Blanche most pronouncedly, either by distinction of clothing or by pronounced makeup or elaborate hairstyle?

Clairemarie Verheyen: Blanche always had focus—if for no other reason than the blonde wig—regardless of her clothing. But remember, I was not involved in any way with *Streetcar*.

Question: One final comment: In the spring of 1996, at the staging of the latest Albee Workshop play, *Double Wide*, the characters' "look" helped us identify their natures.

Clairemarie Verheyen: My students did those. I was in on it—I consulted with them. They wanted the characters to look very contemporary, to look New York, and they wanted to show them as striving to be up-wardly mobile.

Question: Several had distinctly opposite characteristics. One of the women looked shy and reserved; another blabbed constantly. Did these factors give you and your students any clues on clothing them?

Clairemarie Verheyen: I think the one was much more aggressive than the other, and my students would have known it from the script. They chose pants for her; for the other, they dressed her in a very sweet, de-mure, quiet, retiring wallflower print—in essence, a conservative, small-print dress.

Question: What about the mother?

Clairemarie Verheyen: The mother was in sort of an ensemble, a "Sears Special"—the type of dress that people who don't have a lot of money but who want to look well-dressed would wear. She wants desperately to join the upper class, but she is very middle American class.

Question: Your students, then, were not only astute in reading and analyzing the script but also creative in moving the characters to the stage.

Clairemarie Verheyen: Of course. They had investigated the playwright's clues in the script!

Notes from Lecture by Set Designer Kevin Rigdon

Designer Kevin Rigdon, of Houston's Alley Regional Theatre, shared his concepts on the designer-director relationship in a guest appear-ance at a class session of the University of Houston's School of The-atre, Houston, Texas, on 23 April 1996. Before joining the staff at the Alley, Rigdon designed many Broadway productions, among them *The Crucible, Grapes of Wrath,* and *Speed the Plow.* He was also asso-ciated with the Steppenwolf Theatre Organization for more than a decade.

How can the designer and director create a constructive relationship in production? Rigdon suggested that the director and designer should begin their initial meetings with a dialogue whose purpose is to establish the routine of exchanging basic concepts.

At the first actual production meeting, the designer might come in with visual images (not graphic yet) that may be appropriate for the show, formed from his recent reading of the script. But at the outset, the de-signer might first ask the director, "Why did you choose this particular play?" Rigdon gave an example of one director's choice of Steinbeck's *Grapes of Wrath* that he intended to produce in Israel. Rigdon had been intrigued by the prospect and accepted. The first question he asked the director at their meeting was, "Why did you choose this particular play?" The director said, "It's very appropriate to Israel today!" Rigdon expressed doubt, so the director took him at once to a resettlement camp to look at Ethiopian Jews who had lost all. Seeing them, Rigdon agreed that *Grapes of Wrath* was a story that could be told there.

At a second designer-director meeting, a designer may have his design ideas conceptualized. Although many directors would still want only verbal suggestions at these initial discussions, sometimes the designer might bring with him pictures, photos, and design concepts. Rigdon might take with him photos of people with an interesting quality of light on them, in black and white, matching the mood of characters in the script. For a contemplated production of *One Flew Over the Cuckoo's Nest*, Rigdon once brought to an early meeting a book of pictures showing a Greek mental asylum with patients sprawled on the straw in a ceramic structure.

On one unusual occasion, a Rigdon director brought his own design-materials to a meeting and presented them; but after Rigdon explained his own concepts, the director swept all of his own materials off onto the floor and accepted the designer's plans instead. Another director, for a production of *Antony and Cleopatra*, wanted graffiti on the set's walls. Rigdon did not agree, feeling that the graffiti would appear "fake," and suggested instead that deep scratches on the walls would be more appropriate. This director ultimately accepted his designer's view.

It is vital not to let the director come to early discussions and say, "This is what I want to do." That is treating the designer as a draftsman. Preferable would be for the director to come in and talk about the play itself; this approach lets the designer be creative. To Rigdon, it is "absolutely frustrating" to have a director outline specifically at the outset what he wants to do with design. Why? For one, a designer naturally wants to get some of the artistic credit for the design when the reviews for the play appear. After these early dialogues, the designer can put together his or her complete design concept. Rigdon himself starts by visualizing a blank stage, then imagining a person coming in a door. This process helps him approach the next meeting with a more complete though still rough concept. Eventually, the design itself materializes in his mind.

A big part of the designer's job is "listening" in order to foster "give and take" among playwright, director, and designer. Rigdon calls this exchange "dialogue." Some playwrights, however, have ironfisted ideas of what they want—and a few may actually be unable to rewrite. With many, designers can have a productive dialogue. Most designers prefer to have their first meetings with the director and playwright alone, not with costumer, sound engineer, or other designers who often want at once to get down to nuts and bolts. But later, after initial concept meetings, Rigdon likes to take ideas from other designers, too. He sees a close relationship between costuming and lighting design. Naturally, the lighting designer comes into rehearsals later than the costumer; because the lighting designer thinks spatially, he is extremely helpful in shaping and blocking.

What can a designer do if the design budget is too limited to cover what the script needs? Even on a shoestring budget, nothing is totally out of reach. For example, a designer does not need steam coming out of a hole on stage, nor does one need a thousand lights to create a stage picture; imagination is the answer. Rigdon himself is a minimalist; he finds that huge sets override the actors. *Angels in America* had too big a stage; it lost the actors. He likes the effect of one chair on a barren stage.

More importantly, a designer needs a way of handling people. The designer must not be belligerent; must work with people; has to be part of "the answer," not simply announce, "I want this or that"; must figure out how; may have to compromise or to balance if he or she can't win the case. The designer must reach a solution—an answer. How? The designer must remember that some things just don't seem to matter in moving the play along, so the designer can omit them. Rigdon gives an example from his "compromise" design for *Julius Caesar*. At first he had demanded a pool of blood for Caesar's death scene; but he admitted that it would be impractical and messy to clean up after. So he used his imagination and settled upon just letting the conspirators dip their hands in blood as an appropriate compromise, and he was satisfied with the result.

Speaking of his preferred type of theatre, Rigdon advocates those that are easy to design for. His favorite was a meat-and-potatoes theatre that had five rows, five hundred seats, and a low stage, making designing simple. He has found the nontraditional structure of the Alley Theatre challenging; even after considerable work, the structure may still impose itself on the design.

In conclusion, Rigdon recommends that imagination and curiosity are essential for designers. Curiosity about other disciplines—science and architecture, for example—feeds imaginations. If he had it to do again, he would major in architecture, a field that would serve a designer superbly.

13

The Designer's Interaction with the Theatre Team

REGIONAL THEATRE: COSTUMER CARYN NEMAN, *ANGELS IN AMERICA*, 1996

In 1996, designer Caryn Neman worked with the actors in Tony Kushner's *Angels in America*, directed by Michael Wilson at Houston's Alley Theatre. Her work helped the actors project their roles to the audience.

Belize (Michael McElroy), who does "drag," looked his part in the glitzy garb designed for him by costumer Neman. The staid business suits of Joe Pitt (David Whalen), the inhibited but bisexual Mormon, instantly spoke to us of the character's initial discomfort in the arms of gay Louis. Actor Pitt's ultraconservative look convinced us, too, that before his character's gay sprint, he could well have written far-right tracts for Cohn, his rigid McCarthyite boss. And Neman's skill did not let us miss the flakiness of Harper (Annalee Jefferies), wrapping her in blanketlike clothes that played up her imbalance and lack of image. When her attire changed to "svelte" much later, the switch made us aware that Harper was regaining her esteem and her will to live. Neman's choice of attire for Prior Walter (John Feltch)—a long cape and hood—gave him an appropriate monklike look, thoughtful and serene, when his character seemed to accept his angel-appointed role of prophet. Later, when he seemed to receive "the gift of grace"—a bit more life—his sprightly clothing matched his lighter demeanor and supplied us with hope that he, like his friends, would make some progress toward love and joy in life.

The costumer's skill was evident in each distinguishing detail of dress; her work gave viewers an instant clue to the character's present emotional or physical state, supplementing the actors' internal embodiment of the role.

ACADEMIC THEATRE: SCENIC DESIGNER JONATHAN MIDDENTS, FOR SAMUEL BECKETT'S *HAPPY DAYS*

The setting for Samuel Beckett's *Happy Days* at the University of Houston's School of Theatre, 1993, suited flawlessly the script's doomed world in which Beckett housed his desolate humans. Technical designer Jonathan Middents and director Edward Albee's collaboration met the School's high standards for mounting serious theatre.

The interaction of director and designer placed on stage a set appropriate for the stagnant world in which Beckett's two stymied characters, Winnie and Willie, will be contained. With Middents' care for Beckett's intent, the stage becomes a desert, its focal point an amber mound of realistic striation. Yet in protracted daylight, this barren space attracts rather than repels viewers watching Beckett's Winnie and Willie struggle to endure their lot within its hot light. (Even harsher for the two might have been an eternal dark—an alternative with which Beckett had experimented for several other plays' stagings.) This hot void helps actress Patricia Kilgarriff simulate for audiences the irony of Winnie's view of her life as she counts her blessings, sighing, "What I find so wonderful . . . so many tender mercies . . . air, light, warmth!" The height and grimness of the stage-filling mound make it conceivable to viewers that actor James Belcher, playing Willie, can hide behind the mound to avoid Winnie's chatty violation of his peace. She can hear only vaguely his surly sounds or syllables when she eggs him into responding to her rambling.

Striking stage properties add movement to the bleak atmosphere: A music box plays "The Merry Widow Waltz" with bell-like resonance; a parasol self-ignites and bursts into flame; a mirror and a bottle of tonic crash with a perfect match of sound to action. Winnie needs the music box and parasol to busy herself when her recurring phobia, fear of unscheduled time, threatens her sanity.

The design of the mound, with its breadth and thickness, makes it believable that, as Winnie tells the viewers, Willie can slither in and out of a hole at the rear of the mound, lumbering along with what she, immobile, demeans as his stupid mobility. The illusion that she describes provides the audience with the sense of action—of Willie lowering his head and crouching his back to enter and exit his hole to fill his own long days. Even with both characters, as a rule, inert, the end result of the set and its properties is to keep the play moving. The strong scenic design and pseudodynamic characterization in this reputedly abstruse Beckett work lay to rest frequent critical complaints that *Happy Days*, though it may be a sound piece of literature, lacks true theatricality.

PART V
THE ACTOR

14

The Actor's Role

As the curtain rises, audiences respond to actors immediately and vividly. Being so instantly perceived, each actor must help the audience link him or her to the appearance, voice, and manner of the character the actor represents.

To clinch audience perception of the actor as the playwright's scripted character, the actor will need to study the script and subtext for clues to his character's "person." Interaction with other members of the production's theatre team helps the actor take a role from the author's page to the stage, imitating the scripted character's manner of standing, walking, talking, sitting, and even more difficult, investing himself/herself gradually with the character's thoughts, beliefs, and mannerisms (Cohen 1983, 6). Having envisioned and internalized the character's physical and psychological aspects (what the character hopes, fears, values), the actor will become the scripted character for those in the audience.

To undergo this metamorphosis, each actor needs the support of the director, other actors, and designers as rehearsals move the script toward dramatic performance. Each actor can use rehearsal sessions to catch the reactions of the other actor to whom he directs his lines; these instant reactions will offer the speaker hints to the effectiveness of his delivery— of his vocal tone and body language. The director's suggestions, too, can give actors increasing skill in projecting meaning and feeling into their roles. Through this rehearsal-interaction, intrinsic to the art of acting, the actors will develop much-coveted inner confidence in their own performance.

Though the responsibility for these improvements in performance is both director's and actor's, the burden can be lightened when actors approach the stage motivated to work. A producer of note has facetiously suggested that a problem with a small percentage of actors is that "they think they can go on stage and not work, not perform, and [yet] be 'overheard' by the audience" (Dunlop 1990, 100). The same producer vows, "Voice teaching is absolutely appalling all over the world. . . . People are conned by voice teachers who are training actors to make wonderful noises like AAAAHHH"; he insists that "the sound is not what conveys the meaning of the lines the actors are saying" (Dunlop 1990, 100). He wants to hear, primarily, consonants—not "beautiful words." Consonants not only carry the meaning but make it easy for an actor to be heard in a very big theatre (Dunlop 1990, 100).

Another criticism actors sometimes hear must be puzzling—that their speech is too regional or that it is so "standard mid-America" that it is flat and colorless: "Speech training in America really kills interesting ways of speaking, in order to get uniformity" (Michael Kahn, quoted in Loney 1990, 106). Yet chaos would result in a staging with "one Southerner, one Texan, one Californian, and one New Yorker all speaking with a different ear for dialect" (Michael Kahn, quoted in Loney 1990, 106).

With collaborating actors testing and perfecting their speaking skills in rehearsal and, ultimately, projecting their roles in performance, the audience feels what the scripted characters feel—hate, love, despair, elation. Thus the audience gets from drama the benefit of emotional jarring—as playwrights often intend.

15

Interviews, Personal Comments, Points of View

Kathleen Butler's Reflections on Preparing a Role

Ms. Butler, a professional actress, starred in Edward Albee's premiere production of *Three Tall Women* at the Vienna (Austria) English Theatre, 1991, and in the production at the Alley (Houston, Texas) Regional Theatre, 1994.

A successful production comes about only when every artist—director, actor, designers, stage managers et al.—completely and harmoniously carry out their respective roles. It is the happiest and most satisfying event in theatre. What follows are some thoughts on how we as actors can fulfill our responsibility in this collaborative process.

BEFORE THE FIRST DAY OF REHEARSAL

Read the play—read it again, and again—as many times as possible. Pick up the playwright's rhythms and language, find the arc of the play (its dramatic action and the interaction of all its characters) and how your character fits into the play as a whole.

Try to memorize the lines by rote before beginning rehearsal. It is pure drudgery and no one likes to do it, but there are benefits. It enables you to spend valuable rehearsal time actually looking at and reacting to your fellow actors—interacting without worrying about lines. And, fair warning, with the increasingly short rehearsal periods in some of the financially strapped LORT theatres, every minute must be used to its fullest advantage.

When an actor learns by rote, he usually learns verbatim. This is crucial. Paraphrasing is nonprofessional, a despicable habit; it also makes for very sloppy acting. With a good or great playwright, any word out of place jumps out at the audience and jars the rhythm of the play. Mr. Albee once asked me after a run-through of *Marriage Play* whether I had said "and" in a particular line. He then buried his head in his script and said: "I'm sure I wrote 'but'! Yes, I did write 'but' . . . I thought so!" I rolled my eyes, but of course he was absolutely right. I had changed the meaning of the line with one word.

Finally, if you learn your lines beforehand, you won't have to spend evenings trying to memorize when your mind may be tired from long rehearsal hours—it frees you to devote your evenings to homework.

THE REHEARSAL PROCESS

First and foremost: KEEP AN OPEN MIND! Take the time to stop, look and listen to those around you. You don't have to love them, you don't even have to like them, but you do have to work with them. This does not mean that you must sacrifice artistic integrity—but you are all working toward the same end and that's what's important!

The first days of rehearsal are usually devoted to reading the play. Perhaps the word "reading" is misleading. From Day One, communicate the meaning of what you are saying—what the playwright has you saying. Form a bond with your fellow actors, use them and let them use you. An actor's best and primary prop on stage is another actor. The rehearsal period is, above all, a time for growth, experimentation, creativity and all those good things we actors love. Have fun, be inventive, be brave! Learn from doing!

It is the actor's job to create an inner life and a physical life for his character. The two "lives" evolve simultaneously—one feeds off the other. It is the marriage of the two "lives" that brings the role alive and makes it full and believable.

THE INNER LIFE

The goal of the actor is to put images and intentions into the playwright's words, to underscore dialogue with thought and feeling. Work for clarity of each phrase and each word. Learn to love the words and make them part of your character.

Whatever you do as the character must evolve from the material in the text. The best and purest sources of emotion are suggested in the lines and the circumstances of the play. This, however, leaves a great deal of leeway for the actor's creativity. Making provocative and evocative choices will enhance and fill the moment and work for the play as a whole. In *Three Tall Women*, the character "B" uses the phrase "Let it be" several times during Act I when speaking to "C." Is "B" trying to squash "C" by telling her in effect to shut up? Is "B" trying to alert "C" and keep her out of harm's way with "A"? Is "B" trying to use those words to poke fun at "C" for her own amusement? Is "B" smoothing things over so everything stays on an even keel?—and on and on. The choices are almost limitless. The use of the figurative words "squash," "alert," "poke," "smooth," stimulate imagination. Margaret in *Henry VI*, Part 3, in an effort to ridicule the captured York, presents him with a blood-soaked cloth that has been drenched with his dead young son's blood and says:

> Look York: I stain'd this napkin with the blood
> That valiant Clifford, with his rapier's point
> Made issue from the bosom of the boy
> And if thine eyes can water for his death,
> I give thee this to dry thy cheeks withal.

What is she really doing with those words? One choice: Is she trying to pierce York's own heart with her cruelty in order to crush him like a bed bug? The words "pierce" and "crush him like a bed bug" put an image in the actor's mind; by selecting and playing out those strong intentions, the actor brings power and clarity to Shakespeare's words.

By being specific and playing vivid, imaginative intentions, the emotion comes out of what you're doing—you're not just pasting it on. The overall intention in Margaret's speech might be "to crush him like a bed bug." Of course, all actors can and do draw on their personal emotional life (their Golden Box) to reinforce an emotion that may be appropriate for a given moment, but that is a personal process that must be carefully controlled.

PHYSICAL LIFE

To create a physical life of his character, an actor has all sorts of "tools" at his disposal. The following are just a few examples.

Props

There are two kinds of props: those called for specifically in the script and those that an actor might choose to illuminate the life of his character.

In Tennessee Williams's *Sweet Bird of Youth*, the princess receives a phone call telling her that she is again a star. Obviously the telephone is called for in the script; but the actor must handle the phone in a way that is true to the character at that moment of the play. Does she hold onto it as if it is her life's blood? Does she twirl the cord in a particular way? Does she move around the room and keep getting caught and pulled back by the cord? Does she speak into it as if it were an alien or does she whisper into it as if it were a lover?

Suppose Gertrude in the closet scene in *Hamlet* wears a locket with her dead husband's likeness around her neck. What would that do to the interpretation of the scene? Is Gertrude wearing it to assuage her guilt for being an accomplice in her husband's death? Is she wearing it to manipulate Hamlet into believing she is with him and nothing has really changed? Is she wearing it because she really does mourn the death of her husband? All sorts of possibilities exist within the context of the play. In Miller's *Death of a Salesman*, Linda carries a Brownie box camera on the morning of Biff's big game at Ebbets Field. With it she captures a moment of greatness in the Loman family that will soon be blotted out by tragedy. The camera is not on the prop list, but it evokes special behavior on the part of Linda and the rest of the family. How poignant if that picture is framed somewhere on the set in the Loman home— becoming a wonderful visual aid for the actors!

Costumes

In *Mary of Scotland* by Maxwell Anderson, Elizabeth comes to confront Mary in her prison room at Carlisle Castle. They have never met before. What do these two queens wear—how can it help define their characters? Does Elizabeth dress mainly in white so that her motives appear pure even though she plans to have Mary killed? Or perhaps she wears the strong color of red to reinforce her sense of power. Or she may wear red because she loves the color of blood—especially the blood of those who would be in her way. What about Mary? Would she wear some extraordinary piece of fine cloth to remind Elizabeth that she, too, is a queen? Would she wear a large, ornate crucifix given to her by the Pope or a simple, hand-made [sic] cross as a statement of who she is and what she stands for? Perhaps Mary Tyrone in *Long Day's Journey into Night* wears an old pair of white lace gloves. Are they to cover her hands now crippled with arthritis? Are they the same gloves she wore to the theatre on the evening she met her husband? Are they a subconscious way of keeping her hands away from the soiled life of her family? Choices, Choices, Choices!

Work with the costume designer: [L]isten to what the designer has in mind, come up with ideas of your own and together find what will help you with your characterization.

Makeup

The same holds true with appropriate make up [sic]. Again in *Mary of Scotland*, Mary has been imprisoned. Her look should suggest this; she should not look like a Valley Girl. Perhaps she does not sleep well in prison and has developed dark circles under her eyes. Or possibly she has overrouged herself and done her hair elaborately to present an un-vanquished opponent to the visiting Elizabeth.

Movement

How does a character walk and move about the stage? In June Bing-ham's *Triangles*, the character of Eleanor Roosevelt ages from 28 to 66. The actor is presented with the problem of aging. You can't just play "old age," for instance. It looks phony because no one person ages the same way. The tall, young Eleanor had a wasp waist and full breast. Does she slump because of her shyness? Does she stand with regal bear-ing to face the world with her well-known fortitude? Is she graceful—does she like to dance? As she ages, how does her full figure begin to change? What kind of shoes would she choose for her many duties? By taking into consideration all aspects of a character's life, a believable and unique physical presence will evolve to illuminate the playwright's text.

In the dynamics of the theatre, each actor should maintain his individ-uality; yet the actor must serve the production as a whole. That is the director's function—to bring it all together. The finest directors are not dictators. They have hired you because they expect wonderful things from you. Do those wonderful things—some of them will work, some will not. At the end of each rehearsal or run-through, a director will sit down with the cast and crew and give notes. It's part of the process and there is no escaping. DON'T BE DEFENSIVE! To sit through notes every day and have an actor give every excuse in the book for each note re-ceived is absolutely infuriating to the rest of the company. Listen to what the director has to say, ask him to clarify it if you don't understand, make a note of it in your script, try it the next day; and if there is still a problem, discuss it during rehearsal or privately. If you finally can't do what he asks, come up with something better.

THE RUN OF THE PLAY

In the LORT Theatre [in New York city], the run is usually four weeks. In an open run, if the play is well received, it can go on for months, even years. Once the play has opened, and the actor has laid the groundwork for his role, it's there; you don't have to think about it. It is like a mu-sician who practices measures over and over in a particular piece. Once he begins performing, the audience does not hear the technique—it hears the music. The trick of working in a long run is to go from moment to moment during each performance. By living in the moment, concentrat-ing on what is going on now, your character remains alive, open to everything and everyone around him. This does not mean freedom to do as we please; everything must be within the framework set by the director, but no two performances are the same nor should they be.

The superb Myra Carter originated the role of "A" in *Three Tall Women*. No matter how many performances she did, I would find her pouring over her script in her dressing room—always working to make it better, always looking for the undiscovered gold in that brilliant text. She never stopped, nor should any actor ever stop refining and deepening the work. The actor's goal in a run should be that his last performance is his best.

Actors at Houston's Alley Regional Theatre

The eight actors in Tony Kushner's 1994 Pulitzer Prize–winning play, *Angels in America*, faced stiff challenges to acting skill as they projected their roles to audiences at a 1995 Alley Regional Theatre production. The eight actors portrayed two dozen characters in all. In arresting interviews with theatre critic Everett Evans, each disclosed his/her foremost challenge. Excerpts from Evans's pivotal article, "The Work of 'Angels' " in the *Houston Chronicle*'s Arts Notes column (16 April 1995, sec. D, p. 1, 12) appear here.

Actor James Black (Roy Cohn plus one cameo): "The biggest challenge for me ... is the sheer length of the piece. It's close to seven hours of material. As Roy Cohn, I must maintain a high-pitched intensity throughout the show, right up to his demise. It's taxing physically and mentally" (1).

Actor John Feltch (Prior Walter plus one cameo): "For me, the most challenging part is simply sustaining the physical aspect of Prior's decay from AIDS—and being able to shrug that off when I need to shrug it off" (1).

Actress Betty Fitzpatrick (five roles, including Hannah Pitt and Ethel Rosenberg): "The most challenging part for me (when I play multiple roles) is to bring on a complete character every time I change costumes and come back onstage. Even though you've just exited as one person, you must come back as someone completely different" (1).

Actor Joseph Haj (Louis Ironson plus one cameo): "In terms of my character, the challenging aspect is to not let him come off as a one-dimensional villain, the figure who abandons his lover who's dying of AIDS, but to convey something more complex" (1).

Actress Annalee Jefferies (Harper Pitt plus one cameo): "The challenge for me is to follow Harper's journey from A to Z, an amazing journey for anyone to go through. I have to find that path anew each time, not getting ahead of myself or falling behind, not projecting too early what the end will be. So much of myself has to be brought *into* this process" (2).

Actor Michael McElroy (Belize and Mr. Lies): "[In Part I] the challenge for me is that I have so much down time; it's difficult to come onstage with the energy level that's been set before. [In Part II] the challenge is doing all the stage business of Belize's nursing—handling the TV and all that stuff" (12).

Actor David Whalen (Joe Pitt plus two cameos): "The most challenging aspect for me is the journey Joe goes through—from trying to live dead and numb in his self-deception and loathing, to opening up his heart and soul and being true to what he really is" (12).

Actress Shelley Williams (seven roles, including the Angel and Emily, the nurse): "The challenging aspects for me are to make the Angel as clear an entity as possible and to make each of my seven roles distinct" (12).

(N.B. The actors found rewards for their difficult portrayals in their audiences' positive reception to the production. Actress Shelley Williams summarized her reactions to the playscript and its audience reception thus: "Tony Kushner is presenting some very difficult issues for people to deal with, but he has packaged them in a stunningly beautiful script. So people are coming to this show, facing things that are very difficult to face—and asking the right questions" [12].)

Regional and Community-Theatre Actress
Cyndy Witherspoon

Witherspoon's comments on preparing roles for the Creighton Theatre in Texas and for the Actor's Workshop in Houston.

I have played many roles in community and regional theatres, beginning with Teetotal Tessie in *Deadwood Dick*, Agnes in *Gypsy*, Agnes Gooch in *Mame*, and Dani in *Cementville*. All of the characters were starkly different from each other.

I had to get into each one's mind, actually make myself believe that I knew what the character was thinking. That is difficult to do when I cannot even read my best friend's mind—or my own Mother's! Aid does not always appear in the script. Interpretation by the director is of the utmost importance. A good playwright and a good director + good casting = success! Interaction with other cast members at rehearsal also helps me read the character's mind. I can judge much from their reactions to my character's lines and body movements.

Putting my vivid imagination into play also helps me identify with the character whom I portray.

Actors can always tell when the audience is "dead," not responding to their character. Viewers become "dead" if the actors are only "going through the motions." We need to give our characters LIFE! Some experienced actors say that to be convincing, I must "eat, sleep and breathe" the role. Each of us must feel the part to know which actions should be strongly emphasized. The actor who can "feel" certain things will be able to make suggestions to the director about how to deliver her lines. The director is a competent reinforcer of confidence for us. Directors know in their mind's eye what they want, and are excellent conveyers of help to us. The director may not be infallible, but he is sensitive and creative and generous in helping us enrich our roles. I would love to expound on the director, but have never "walked a mile in his shoes." I know his job is incredibly painstaking, time-consuming and tedious.

A difficult form of acting for me is the delivery of a soliloquy. As I speak the passage, I must interact, not with the other actors, but with the audience. It is crucial to be totally natural in a soliloquy yet to relate closely with those beyond the footlights. I need hours of rehearsal time to perfect the delivery of a soliloquy. Another difficulty for me is the need to remain in control when cues go astray. Cues are everything; it is when they are delayed or missed out that I need to be prepared to forge ahead promptly and smoothly.

Study has much to do with developing a role. First, I read the script thoughtfully, trying to visualize it on stage. As I memorize the lines, I try to add a gesture or two, incorporating them into my delivery. I think it is essential for me to know the lines so well that at rehearsal, I can go back to any scene when asked, without confusion.

Sometimes it's really hard to stay "in character" during a performance. If I don't like the character I am portraying, it is even more difficult. That's where I actually have to get into heavy acting. I have tried all methods of staying in character. Sometimes I stay in my costume for a time before a performance. At other times I speak in whatever dialect I have mastered for the role. It helps that in essence, by nature, we are all actors; we put on different faces to different people, and almost become the personality we pretend. Though we, in our human pretenses, sometimes lose sight of who we are, we can usually carry it off without total confusion. Just so, we must keep our on-stage [sic] pretense firm. Our biggest help here is the director. He can take us back to the character again and again in rehearsal. Together the director and I have created the character during rehearsal, making it as close to the playwright's vision as we can. Directors, after all, are a great support system for us. We are all—director, cast and crew—striving for the same goal: to move this script to the audience and convince them it is real.

16

The Actor's Interaction with the Theatre Team

ZOE CALDWELL

Since the 1950s, when Zoe Caldwell began her acting career, she has dedicated herself to enhancing the quality of live theatre. Caldwell has constantly honed her emotional, vocal, and physical powers (Roberts, Robertson, and Barranger 1989, 110). On Broadway, in 1996, she received the Antoinette Perry (Tony) Award for her performance as the Greek opera singer Maria Callas in Terrence McNally's *Master Class* (1995).

To interviewers seeking Zoe Caldwell's acting secrets and principles, she has said with a facetious grin, "Of course you've got to speak loudly enough so that the audience can hear you, and you've got to remember your lines. . . . [But] there are absolutely no rules in this business" (Tierney 1970, 20). For Caldwell, an open mind toward playwright's intent and to changes in acting style receive more stress than "rules." However, an analysis of her published comments on the art of acting reveal, if not rules, the lucid processes by which she has developed her roles during her decades in theatre.

Her prime emphasis has remained on openness to possibilities and points of view—on being flexible in the face of new and diverse acting methods. Another focus has been on increasing her vocal range, so that she now has a voice which she can raise or drop four out of five registers. The *New York Herald Tribune*'s Walter Kerr (23 June 1961) has described her use of voice thus: "She flatters a man at nightingale pitch, then drops her voice to cut his heart out" (quoted in Roberts, Robertson, and Bar-

ranger 1989, 108). Yet another focus has been on pre-rehearsal preparation in order to identify with her character's appearance, style, vocal
range, and, through active research, to determine the character's more
internal characteristics. Using her "acute intelligence and emotional
range," Caldwell has made roles like that of Helena in *All's Well That
Ends Well* into some of "the most moving of Shakespeare's heroines (Roberts, Robertson, and Barranger 1989, 108). She has fashioned the role of
Cleopatra in *Antony and Cleopatra* into "a royal harlot: sexy, foul-mouthed
and funny, itching with desire ... yet royal, too, with the same animal
unselfconsciousness that made her wanton" (Roberts, Robertson, and
Barranger 1989, 109). Aspiring actresses may wish to follow Caldwell's
pattern, expanding their performance range to cover diverse acting
modes in both tragedy and comedy, in ancient and modern classics. From
the outset, Caldwell's drive has been to make each role a success through
sound preparation. She has commented, shuddering, "Obviously one
wouldn't want to be laughed off the stage by one's peers" (Tierney 1970,
58).

Caldwell has also said, "I do like to be able to identify closely with a
character"; her bent for characterization of women who have lived rather
than those of purely fictional derivation has drawn critical attention to
her roles on stages in England, Canada, Australia, and the United States
(Tierney 1970, 20). To form each of these characterizations, she scrutinizes
the script, plumbs its subtext, then adds factual background by intensive
research into the lives of the women she plays. Throughout this research,
she addresses her imagination to the information she gains.

Caldwell has shared details with interviewers on how she obtains this
background for her roles, on what assists her most in making inferences
about the characters' situations, expectations, traits, standards. "I enjoy
working on the background," she has said; "I like to identify closely with
a character" (Tierney 1970, 20). Long before rehearsals, she has begun
her preparation. To develop the title role of *Colette* in 1968, she went to
France. "I visited Colette's birthplace and other spots that meant a lot to
her. I met people who played a big part in her life, like her daughter
and her third husband" (Tierney 1970, 20). For a later role in Terence
Rattigan's *A Bequest to the Nation*, Caldwell learned that during the period
treated in the play, her character, Lady Hamilton, had put on excessive
weight from bouts of drinking; with this data, the actress deliberately
gained added weight to simulate Lady Hamilton's actual appearance.
She also worked to develop a Lincolnshire accent like that of her character.

Developing a role's more internal characteristics has also been the focus of Caldwell's discourse. She refers to this process as an actress's vital
responsibility: "If you don't do that, you're not an actor. But it is hard
to be specific because it is a sort of mystery process that happens deep

in the subconscious" (Tierney 1970, 20). Critics, seeing the results of this "mystery process" in the portraits she creates on our stages, write that even in her earliest seasons of Shakespeare in the 1950s, her carefully wrought and delivered portrayals of Bianca to Paul Robeson's Othello, Cordelia to Charles Laughton's King Lear, and Helena in Tyrone Guthrie's production of *All's Well That Ends Well* had been "particularly noteworthy"; critics felt that these performances "singled her out as one who can speak verse not only as though she both means it and understands it but in such a way that it seems perfectly to express all the subtlety, flow, and depth of her feelings" (Roberts, Robertson, and Barranger 1989, 107).

By the 1990s, critics had affixed the term "legendary" to Caldwell's name (Leithauser, *Time* [10 November 1995]). During her career to date, three Tony Awards have came to her for acting artistry: 1966's Tennessee Williams's play *Gnadiges Fraulein*, directed by Alan Schneider; 1968's *The Prime of Miss Jean Brodie*; and fourteen years later, Robinson Jefferson's adaptation of *Medea*. Since those awards, critics have predicted that "other significant acting achievements may be expected from this actress in the future" (Roberts, Robertson, and Barranger 1989, 110). *Newsweek's* Jack Kroll suggested that Caldwell's Maria Callas in McNally's *Master Class* is one to remember, one that's certain to sweep every award in the business" (13 November 1995). She has developed Callas as a "tremulous woman whose fame provides some compensation for, but little insulation from, heartbreak" (Leithauser, *Time* [10 November 1995]). She plays the opera star not as a singer of world renown, but "as a wise-cracking, washed-up Callas . . . a superficial opera-queen fantasy figure" (Davis 1995, 89). Caldwell depicts Callas's downfall during two extended flashbacks into her loss of voice, her plunge into café society, and her involvement with famous figures like Onassis (Davis 1995, 89). The performance leads the *New York Post's* Clive Barnes to write that McNally has been "lucky, or savvy enough to find in Zoe Caldwell the perfect actress to make his Callas live, breathe, infuriate, and enchant" (6 November 1995). *New York's* John Simon says Caldwell's assiduous work in characterization has brought the role of Callas to the stage in a "more than usually successful tour de force" by reason of her "technique, artistry, boldness, and eclat" (20 November 1995, p. 88).

With her Callas role, actress Zoe Caldwell has again followed the "mystery process" that she has detailed to interviewers: "When you're giving a good performance there's a fine line you can cross where you become almost another person, but still that person is infused with your own lifeblood" (Tierney 1970, 20). During the process of creating this other person, Caldwell experiences "a feeling of death"; yet she adds, "in a way that's good, because it usually happens just before this 'other person' gets created" (Tierney 1970, 20).

EQUITY ACTORS PATRICIA KILGARRIFF AND JAMES BELCHER

Synchronizing Movement and Speech

Consummate skill and sustained rehearsal are sometimes needed to bring a scene to audiences as the script specifies. When an academic venue tackles a classic work for a full-scale production, professional actors may be brought in, first, to supplement the cast of student actors, and second, to teach by example. At the School of Theatre, University of Houston (1993), Equity actors Patricia Kilgarriff and James Belcher played Winnie and Willie in Samuel Beckett's *Happy Days*. For their roles, Kilgarriff and Belcher had to synchronize, without benefit of eye contact, their characters' movements and responses as Kilgarriff stares stage-forward and Belcher faces stage-rear.

One winces at the hours of dedicated rehearsal needed to perfect this timing, with each actor outside the other's direct line of vision, before and behind the set's huge mound of sand. Unfailingly, Belcher and Kilgarriff handle this intricate stage business wherein a second's difference could make or mar its timing. During these stage minutes, a postcard that Willie holds up to examine must be snatched from his lifted fingers by Winnie; she studies it, then disdainfully tosses it back over the mound, at which point it reappears without a second's delay in Willie's fingers as he holds it to his eyes for further scanning. Beckett's intent is clearly conveyed: in their doomed world, the two are souls out of sight of each other, yet in communion.

With another firm draw on acting skill and artistry, Kilgarriff and Belcher stay in character in a final, critical scene when Willie must creep round the mound to center-front stage where Winnie will, for the first time in the play's action, glimpse his body. The actors must stay within the text's map of futility and its hard vision of human existence; yet Beckett's stage directions note that viewers should see a trace of a smile on Kilgarriff's face when, buried to her shoulders in the mound, she catches Willie's shadow. The challenge for Kilgarriff is that Winnie's face and voice must register concomitantly both her joy at Willie's approach and her fear of his motive. Belcher's acting test comes when his body must slither stolidly round the mound into view with his face dispassionate, then painfully arch and stretch as he attempts to ascend the mound. The actors, with rehearsal refining of voice and body movement, stay in character. Kilgarriff shows us her character's confusion: Is he coming round, as she wants to believe, for a kiss from her lips, or for "a something else"—perhaps for the trigger of the old gun that has long been part of their desolate landscape, still resting high on the mound's rough surface toward which Willie reaches. Will he put himself out of his misery, or will he put her out of hers?

With dramatic effect at curtain, Winnie's face bears a haunting smile—of peace? of surcease? Though Beckett's enigmatic ending taunts viewers, its artistic presentation by Kilgarriff and Belcher appeases them.

ACTORS IN DENVER'S REGIONAL THEATRES, 1995 TO THE PRESENT

Of the body of actors who move authors' characters from script to stage, the following four, well known to audiences in the 1990s in Denver's large theatre community, seem representative in their rehearsal preparation of roles. The following remarks are excerpted from "Old Reliables Light Denver Stages," an informative and significant article by drama critics Jeff Bradley and Sandra Brooks-Dillard, published in the *Denver Post* (8 October 1995), sec. E, p. 2.

Gwen Harris

Actress Gwen Harris, who won a Denver Drama Critics Circle nomination for 1994–1995, has worked with three local theatre groups—Eulipions (Denver's predominantly black theatre), City Stage Ensemble, and Theatre on Broadway. Harris's comments show her clear communication with director, playwright, and other actors and her responsibility for full development of characters. During rehearsals of her role in *Five Tellers Dancing in the Rain* for Theatre on Broadway, she faced an inherent hurdle for her in the author's text.

As rehearsals began, Harris found that the character she played was very difficult for her because, as critics have implied, playwright Mark Dunn wrote the role specifically for a white woman (sec. E, p. 2). As Harris rehearsed the lines of the script, she realized that her delivery of the dialogue was not ringing true. The actress recalls stopping often as she spoke a line or two to say to the other actors, "Wait a minute"; then, looking directly at them, she would protest, "I'm a black woman and I wouldn't say that" (sec. E, p. 2). The others listened to her and agreed. With their encouragement, Harris cautiously offered suggestions for wording that seemed less idiomatically narrow, hence more credible for her. Her preferences were also both reasonable and accurate for the nature of the character as scripted. Not only was her counsel accepted at once by the director, but many of her suggested revisions of word and phrase were retained by the playwright in the ultimate script.

To prepare another recent role, that of Nairobi, homeless AIDS victim and hearing-disabled drug-user in *The Raft of the Medusa* at the Theatre on Broadway, Harris's sense of responsibility led her to learn sign language before rehearsals. She needed to sensitize herself to her character's hearing handicap. The actress has asserted, in interviews, that before she plays any role, she "always puts a lot of research into the character" (sec. E, p. 2). As the hard-of-hearing Nairobi, she tested her facial expressions and vocal pitches during rehearsals until the reactions of the other actors showed her she was convincing as a hearing-impaired character. During the subsequent run of the play, her portrayal of Nairobi was deemed exceptional by the press, and the play was well received by its audiences.

Harris has phrased her standard artistic goal sensitively: "I always hope to tap somebody, to affect somebody" (sec. E, p. 2).

Jason Hauser

Another Drama Critics Circle Award recipient, Jason Hauser, a graduate of the University of Colorado's Theatre Department, is now in New York City, acting Off-Broadway. Hauser, whose Denver roles included the drifter in *Picnic*, the prosecutor in *Execution of Justice*, and the horse of the title in *Strider*, recently recalled his last experience in the Colorado Shakespeare Festival as one that led him to rehearsal-interaction of an unusually dramatic nature. The occasion for this unique collaboration came in Hauser's portrayal of General Aufidius in the Festival's production of *Coriolanus*, which Hauser later vowed was "the hardest role I ever had to do" (sec. E, p. 3).

The stress arose as Hauser and the actor playing Coriolanus prepared for their roles by envisioning and internalizing the physical and psychological nature of their respective characters. Studying the roles of the two warriors, the actors gradually became aware of a credibility problem for audiences who would watch battle scenes between Aufidius and Coriolanus. The difficulty could arise from the acute difference in physique between Hauser (playing General Aufidius) and actor David Drummond (playing Coriolanus). Shakespeare's dialogue draws the two roles clearly, with lines in which Coriolanus refers to Aufidius as his equal as a warrior. For Aufidius, Shakespeare's script holds speeches in which the general boasts of his drive to bring down Coriolanus. Because the actor playing Coriolanus (David Drummond) was a massive, six feet six inches, with Hauser of much smaller stature and build, the staging problem was acute: how to manage the battle scenes between the two characters without the effect appearing ludicrous to the audience.

With deliberation and inspiration, it was decided (indeed, conceded) that if people throughout time could accept the David-and-Goliath battle, legendary or not, certainly the trick here could be to have Hauser use exaggeration to make himself as small as possible in stance and to present David Drummond as a modern Goliath. The actors worked at the effect, with Hauser not only "shrinking down" his own bearing but also developing a bizarre fight-style that could compensate for his small physique and explain this small David's prowess. The stratagem worked, and their battles "provided some of the festival's most exciting moments" (sec. E, p. 3).

The audience's reaction to the Hauser and Drummond interaction pleased both actors and led Hauser to say of theatre, "For me, as an actor, there are personal rewards—that transaction that occurs between [me] and the audience. When a scene really clicks, it can be the most exciting, elating, extravagant sensation" (sec. E, p. 3).

Jacqueline Antaramian

Actress Jacqueline Antaramian credits the existence of repertory groups for her opportunity to interact closely with director, designer, and other actors. In her three years of summer stock at Donovan Marley's Pacific Conservatory of the Performing Arts, and in her seven years with the Denver Center Theatre Company (DCTC), also headed by Donovan Marley, the actress has had the occasion to know well the core of repertory actors with whom she collaborates. As she works with them, she says, "Respect grows, trust grows, and therefore the work grows, and we hope the audience can feel that" (sec. E, p. 3).

This intense communication and involvement during rehearsal helped her develop her roles in plays such as *Hedda Gabler, Candide, Miss Julie, Romeo and Juliet,* and *The Rose Tattoo.* The result she works toward is an embodiment of her characters so fully that her audience will feel that she is, indeed, the character she is playing. Her years with the group, preparing these roles for performance, mastering the art of staying in character from start to finish of each separate performance, gave her confidence, teaching her not to be afraid of responsibility (sec. E, p. 3). When the DCTC built its 1995–96 season around her, she said, "It makes you feel good that they entrust the work to you" (sec. E, p. 3).

Antaramian denies that acting is "as easy as one might perceive it to be"; it requires "moving an audience, one-on-one, being in the same room, as opposed to film or TV" (sec. E, p. 3). This need to stir an audience reflects the Denver Center Theatre Company's rationale for existence. Their success in rousing their viewers into awareness, or, as Antaramian phrases it, into "thinking about something," into feeling *something* "so long as it's not apathy," derives from the group's rehearsal effort and is what this actress finds "most rewarding in the repertory experience" (sec. E, p. 3). Through her association with acting companies, Antaramian feels that she has enjoyed "the beauty of what theater can do" (sec. E, p. 7).

Tony Church

For the past seven years, character actor Tony Church, founding member of England's Royal Shakespeare Company in 1960, has been the Dean of the Denver Center Theatre Company's National Theatre Conservatory. During 1995, Dean Church, whom critics consider a consummate performer, acted with his students in *King Lear*, unobtrusively modeling for them the skills and techniques that project a playwright's characters to audiences.

Dean Church, with "a poet's understanding of the English Language" (Giffin 1995, 2E), places his emphasis in play production on his actors' total immersion in the playwright's text in order to give a performance that carries the poetry of theatre. As Church and his actors work through a script, he stresses a complete understanding of the dialogue, an imaginative stretch into its subtext, and a meticulously correct delivery of both. He calls for exhaustive preparation "of all schematic work and rehearsal" (sec. E, p. 2). When student actors focus on their roles during rehearsal and performance, he advises them to use imagination, to draw on their vision and creativity. Their efforts will draw up material from the script's subtext: "Every time you play a part, it expands your imagination because you've got to bring your imagination to it—and it feeds back, so you see more and understand more about life and about people" (sec. E, p. 2).

As the group of actors prepare the play, this ardent use of vision will be "wonderfully exhilarating physically," Church tells them, for the "adrenaline-rush" that results from creating a pure "moment of acting" is of huge benefit for actors' bodies" (sec. E, p. 2). Actors, he says, "tend to live longer and be fitter than most other people without taking violent exercise" (sec. E, p. 2). In performance, when his actors are wholly caught up in their delivery of the playwright's speech and action, Church guarantees that "every centimeter of (each one's) body is exercised every minute he's on stage" (sec. E, p. 2). The actors' vigorous entry into the author's script and subtext will create stage moments in which, Church promises, actors can "just let go" and "something bigger than the actor takes over" (sec. E, p. 2). Church affirms, "I believe that" (sec. E, p. 2).

In summary, the superlative moments on stage furnished by actors like Gwen Harris, Jason Hauser, Jacqueline Antaramian, and Tony Church have led critical and popular audiences in the Denver theatre community to anticipate more and more performances with actors "soaring to new heights in plays that match their talents and challenge their gifts" (sec. E, p. 1).

Appendix: Issues for Discussion in Parts I through V

The following lists of "Issues for Discussion," one for each of this volume's parts, are based upon specific concerns or principles addressed in established theatre texts such as Robert Cohen's *Theatre* (Palo Alto, Calif.: Mayfield Publishing Company, 1983) and Oscar Brockett's *History of the Theatre* (Boston: Allyn and Bacon, 1982). These discussion questions also reflect concerns debated in today's theatre and academic forums.

PART I: PRODUCER ISSUES

1. Who or what determines the amount of time scheduled for development of a production? Does it vary with each venue, with the complexity of the playscript, or is it a contractual matter?

2. Who or what influences the selection of the playscript to be developed by the theatre group? Is the decision the producer's?

3. What differences in acting skills appear at auditions for professional, regional, and academic theatre venues? Are the acting skills (as aside from singing or dancing) of actors auditioning for musical roles comparable to those for legitimate theatre?

4. What is the difference between acting a text and acting a lyric?

5. What are the major physical requirements for theatres housing musicals as opposed to nonmusical plays?

6. Does the producer need to provide the singing actor special coaching to make use of the physical, emotional, and vocal systems that enhance performance—breathing, projection, intelligibility?

7. Are significant limitations encountered by regional and academic theatre teams when musical theatre is attempted at facilities without choreographers or music directors? Are such limitations surmountable?

8. With an academic or community theatre, as opposed to a professional venue, would the director need to place more emphasis on perfecting the musical performance than on acting skills?

9. Established musicals like *Fiddler on the Roof* may by contract require use of their original, accepted choreography and staging. Is this at all practical or necessary?

10. How does the producer distribute responsibilities to the staff? How does the producer handle extra responsibilities for the staging of musical numbers?

11. What determines the size and nature of the orchestra or musical group—whether it will be full-sized or limited to the bare bones? (Is its size determined by the type of score, or the size of the budget, the size of the stage, the availability of musicians?)

12. Are producers' jobs made difficult by pay-scale differences for players at different venues?

13. Do scripts that require singers and/or dancers ever have straight acting roles? If so, is the pay scale a problem, and do the actors in each category interact easily—mix well?

14. How much is the structure of musical theatre appearing to alter from its earlier form (re: character development, setting)? How do choruses now serve the musical play?

PART II: DIRECTOR ISSUES

1. With what does the director begin the process of producing a new play? How much discussion with producer or with playwright occurs? With well-established plays (either recent or those in the public domain), how much will previous productions influence the present staging?

2. What or who determines the possible style of production—the use of conventional backdrops, sets, props, or the use of a more abstract and stylistic setting? How much might your choice hinge on whether the playscript was a new or an established production?

3. What or who determines a script's performance tempo—its "flow"? Is it the script or the actors or the director who slows down or speeds up the tempo? To what extent do actors set the tempo naturally by picking up cues, reacting to others' words or actions, slowing down or speeding up?

4. How can the director amplify or modify the author's stage directions for setting, lighting, costumes, properties, characters?

5. Does the director need a scale model of the set before rehearsals

begin? before blocking? What use is made of a scale model in rehearsals, before actual set construction is completed?

6. How much can directors add to sound in staging—wind? storm? slammed doors? weeping? screaming? incidental music? an extra waltz for the dance scene in Williams's *The Glass Menagerie?*

7. Given a choice of facilities (stages) for a new play, how would the director determine the form (type) of stage it should have—traditional, arena, or thrust? Would aesthetics or economics or previous staging determine the choice? (At the Alley's arena staging of *Angels in America*, the director chose an arena staging though the play's Broadway premiere had been on a proscenium stage.)

8. Casting: What role does the director play in selecting the cast? Is it a shared function with producer and playwright?

9. Is it actually possible at auditions to select actors who will fill the script's roles exactly—or is it a long shot? Does a director (often or seldom) need to replace his first choices? How soon might the director be able to realize that his choice had been unfortunate? (Alan Schneider, in *Entrances*, wrote of the tact and trouble that came to him from unfortunate choices of his or of producer/playwright input into casting.)

10. How is the choice of the specific play to be produced usually made? Is it based on budget, on projected audience, on the theatre organization's purpose?

11. Does the financial backer have a part in the decision? In regional theatre, do the artistic director and the managing director have total input?

12. Directors and playwrights frequently resort to the same actors over the years—Mr. Albee has used George Grizzard, Kathleen Butler, Jessica Tandy; Tennessee Williams often used Colleen Dewhurst. Why might a director (and playwright) often choose to work with certain actors again and again? Is it totally from the actors' artistic presence, or perhaps from familiarity with the actors' learning style, concentration span, readiness to accept suggestion (direction?), responsibility, similar concepts of what theatre can or should be, or other considerations? Would it be a money matter?

13. Are the titles "designer" and "draftsman" equally accurate for the responsibility of the persons holding the positions? Do the titles connote the same level of creativity? At what point in production do designers (lighting, sound, costume, set) enter staging?

The Director's Interaction with the Theatre Team

1. What major differences in the sets of circumstances at commercial, regional, or academic theatres might influence the selection of the par-

ticular play and the nature of its production (re: size of budget, theatre space, audience complexion)?

2. How much do differences in time allotted for development of script and for the projected run of the play affect the director's necessary adjustments to staging?

3. Would the director be tied more noticeably to text at professional venues (as in New York City, where the playwright might often be in attendance during negotiations and rehearsals) than at regional or academic theatres?

4. At different types of theatre, are actors usually similar in what they consider appropriate or inappropriate regard for text (re: "duty" to script versus freer interpretation)?

5. At regional or academic venues, can the director make necessary economic adjustments or modifications to scripted stage directions (omit brief lines or scenes) without violating the authority of the text?

6. Is casting handled similarly at various venues, with the same intricacies of contracts or mixes of Equity and non-Equity actors?

7. Is the director's length of commitment to performance after opening somewhat uniform at all venues?

8. Do actors' expertise levels vary discernibly, so that time and extent of direction are factors in the organization's selection of a play and in the probability of its success?

9. Does a director need to be a teacher at one level more than at another, helping actors with tempo, focus, climax, perception of author's characters, and embodiment of that perception for audiences?

10. Does blocking offer more challenge (opportunity for innovation) at one category of theatre than another? How much do factors like size or sophistication of the facility (stage) and the nature of the lighting or of the acoustics predetermine the producer's and director's staging options, complicate their jobs, or limit their artistic drive?

11. How does the availability of support staff (management, technicians, designers) and the extent of consultation with them on set, lighting, sound, and costuming differ at particular venues?

12. With regard to marketing, public relations, and other business matters, to what extent would differences in their handling at a venue alter the preparation of the chosen play?

PART III: PLAYWRIGHT ISSUES

1. Stage directions were often sparse in scripts from past centuries, perhaps because playwrights were expected and welcomed at rehearsals. Today, with playwrights less often present at rehearsals, their scripts tend toward more-explicit stage directions. How might the tendency toward more-explicit stage directions affect our directors, actors, designers?

2. Today, how do playwrights see their role in rehearsals? How far into rehearsal might the playwright wish to attend? How much revision of text would be acceptable with a playwright present?

3. Should today's directors regard scripted stage directions as fixed components of text or as the playwright's "suggestions" for interpreting and performing the script? From the phrase "artistic integrity in production," what might playwrights expect from directors in addition to close adherence to text?

4. After a new play's premiere and first run, might the playwright less often than before approve modifications by the director and team for subsequent productions?

5. How closely do playwrights work with directors and designers on setting? Could a director or designer shift a scene's backdrop and fixed stage pieces from a realistic to an abstract style—or from a simple setting to a busy, involved one?

6. For actors' delivery of dialogue, to what extent are a playright's scripted cues intended as aids for actors? How much might an actor's disregard of scripted cues in favor of his own subjective approach to vocal tone, body language, even dialogue itself, lose the essence of the playwright's intended dramatic experience for the audience? (Can actors be inventive and still simulate and embody the role scripted by the playwright?)

7. With blocking, how vital is the playwright's scripted intention for positioning actors? Can the director move an actor downstage nearer the footlights or further upstage than the text indicates? Would the shifts mar the playwright's intended stage picture?

8. Can stage business or bustling activity not prescribed in the text take away from what the playwright intended for a scene, perhaps spoiling the silent moment during which the audience was to be deeply reflective? Could such shifts mar the rhythm of the scripted lines?

9. Theatre philosophy through the ages has said that playwrights believe that theatre's ultimate worth rests in its arousing and/or redeeming effect on the audience (re: Artaud's wish that it "drain abscesses collectively"). Which elements of production (designers' settings, actors' delivery of lines, or directors' focus on rhythm, sound, and movement) most often fulfill a dramatist's wish to arouse and/or redeem the audience?

PART IV: DESIGNER ISSUES

1. Is it possible to give designers *carte blanche* with design, or do the director and playwright usually have their visions of the setting, lighting, sound, and costuming pretty much in hand at the outset of production sessions?

2. How much does the playwright's script (through its dialogue, stage

directions, action) tell the designer about the appearance the set and costumes should take—whether they should be complex and elaborate or
plain and simple?

3. If abstraction rather than realism is the director's choice in staging
style, can a designer's costuming or scenery still have a dynamic part in
furthering the playwright's intent for his script's staging?

4. Would a designer's work be basically the same for a play staged on
a proscenium stage as on an arena stage? Would adjustments be easy or
difficult?

5. How interrelated are the single components (light, costuming, color,
sound, shape) of the play's design? To what extent does each depend
upon the other? For example, how might lighting and costuming be interrelated?

6. Today, scenic design can be realistic and solid, abstract and fluid,
or a combination of the two. When might a set designer suggest adjustments to a director to enhance or adjust the scripted style?

7. How can lighting serve artistic purposes without becoming a "spectacle" that detracts from the unity of the whole staging?

8. How much does the size of the production's budget limit the designers' tasks? How much can a designer use imagination to solve budget
difficulties in staging?

9. In essence, does the designer serve the playwright rather than the
director? Can dialogue between designer, director, and playwright help
correlate design intents?

PART V: ACTOR ISSUES

1. What assists an actor most in making inferences about the playwright's characters and their situations, expectations, traits, standards?

2. Does aid in apprehending the character's nature appear explicitly
in the script? in its subtext? from the director? from the interaction on
stage during rehearsal? from the actor's imagination?

3. How does the actor decide which actions in the play are major, to
be emphasized more strongly than others? (Does the feeling of priority
[need for emphasis] come when actors first read the play or first interact
with others, or when the designers fix the lighting on them [or on some
stage property]?) Or does this sense of priority come through the director's placement of actor in relation to audience, or to someone or something else?

4. How does interaction with the director or with other actors assist
each actor in noting changes in mood, tempo, character—or in the play
itself?

5. What expedients help actors "get into a role"? Do they devise aids
like eye contact and gestures (shrugs, nods of the head, facial expres-

sions) on their own as they read and memorize lines in the script, or a bit later, with help from the theatre team?

6. How does an actor stay "in character" from start to finish of each separate performance so that the viewers perceive the actor as the character? How do actors maintain the integrity (consistency and continuity) of their characters throughout a long run of the show?

7. From whom do actors seek help if they think the lines they must speak don't ring true to them—sound unnatural or awkward on their tongue—or if the lines don't give them sufficient clues to the person's character, style, and thoughts?

8. How much should actors know about their character? Should they know as much as the director knows—and even more?

9. How can an actor keep a role "fresh"? (Stanislavsky [1948] spoke of the need *before* each performance "not only of a physical make-up but of a spiritual make-up" [460–61].)

Works Cited

Abramson, Mark. "What's It All About, Albee?" Review of *Three Tall Women*. *Woodstock Times* 2 (30 July 1992): 12.

Albee, Edward. Author's Note. *Tiny Alice*. New York: Dramatists Play Service, 1965, p. 5.

——. *The Lorca Play: Scenes from a Life*. Unpublished Manuscript. Copyright 1992.

——. Preface to *Entrances* by Alan Schneider. N.Y.: Viking-Penguin, 1986.

——. Introduction, *Selected Plays of Edward Albee*. New York: Nelson Doubleday, Inc., 1987.

——. National Press Club Address. Moderated by Monroe Karmin. Washington, D.C.: Federal News Service, Inc., 1995.

——. *Three Tall Women*. New York: William Morris Agency, Inc., 1992, 1994. (Published by Audrey Skirball-Kenis Theatre Inc. *Playscript Series*, in *American Theatre* [September 1994].)

Albright, William. Review of *The Lorca Play*. *Houston Post* (18 April 1992), sec. D, p. 2.

"Alley Forum," Houston's Alley Theatre. In Jeane Luere and Sidney Berger, eds. *Playwright versus Director*. Westport, CT: Greenwood Press, 1994.

Artaud, Antonin. *The Theatre and Its Double*. Translated by Mary C. Richards. New York: Grove Press, 1958.

Baker, Christopher. Quoted in Luere and Berger, eds. *Playwright versus Director*. Westport, CT: Greenwood Press, 1994.

Baker, Stephen. Press Release: "Alley Theatre Announces New Managing Director." (14 July 1994).

Barber, John. "Zoe Caldwell." Review of *A Bequest to the Nation* by Terence Rattigan. In *London Daily Telegraph* (25 September 1970). Quoted in Roberts, Robertson, and Barranger. *Notable Women in the American Theatre.* Westport, CT: Greenwood Press, 1989, p. 109.

Barnes, Clive. "In a Class by Herself." *New York Post,* 6 November 1995. Reprinted in *National Theatre Critics' Reviews* 56: 555–56.

Beckett, Samuel. Letter to Alan Schneider. *Beckett at 80/Beckett in Context.* Enoch Brater, ed. New York and Oxford: Oxford University Press, 1986.

Bizet, Georges. *Carmen.* Paris: Calmann, 1838.

Bradbrook, M. C. "Shakespeare Improved." *Staging Shakespeare.* New York and London: Garland Publishing, 1990.

Bradley, Jeff. "London." *Denver Post* (26 November 1950), sec. H, p. 1.

Bradley Jeff, and Sandra Brooks-Dillard. "Old Reliables Light Denver Stages." *Denver Post* (8 October 1995), sec. E, p. 2.

Brady, James. "In Step with Edward Albee." *Parade Magazine* (14 August 1994): 12.

Brantley, Ben. "Edward Albee Conjures Up Three Ages of Woman." Review of *Three Tall Women. New York Times* (14 February 1994), sec. C, p. 13.

Brater, Enoch, ed. *Beckett at 80/Beckett in Context.* New York and Oxford: Oxford University Press, 1986.

Brockett, Oscar. *History of the Theatre.* 4th ed. Boston: Allyn and Bacon, 1982.

Brook, Peter. Introduction to Peter Weiss's *Marat/Sade.* New York: Atheneum Publishers, 1965, p. v.

Brustein, Robert. "Separated by a Common Playwright." Review of Arthur Miller's *Broken Glass.* In *New Republic* 210 (30 May 1994): 22, 29–30.

Canaday, John. "The Artist as Social Critic." *What Is Art?* New York: Random House, 1988.

Canby, Vincent. "A Season of Albee, Obsessions Safely Intact." *New York Times* (20 February 1994), sec. H, p. 5.

Cohen, Robert. *Theatre.* Palo Alto, Calif.: Mayfield Publishing Company, 1983.

Cooke, Richard P. Review of *Cabaret. Wall Street Journal* (22 November 1966), 6.

Copeau, Jacques. "Manifesto for a New Theatre." 1913. Reprinted in Oscar Brockett. *History of the Theatre.* 4th ed. Boston: Allyn and Bacon, 1982, p. 578.

Coven, Brenda, Christine E. King, and Donna M. Albertus. *David Merrick and Hal Prince: An Annotated Bibliography.* New York and London: Garland Publishing, 1993.

Craig, David. *On Singing Onstage.* New York: Schirmer Books, Macmillan Publishing Co., 1978.

Craig, Gordon. *On the Art of Theatre.* New York: Theatre Art Books, 1956.

Davis, Peter G. "The Mythologized Maria." *New York* 28, no. 46 (20 November 1995): 89.

Dunlop, Frank. *Staging Shakespeare: Seminars on Production Problems.* Edited by Glenn Loney. New York and London: Garland Publishing Co., 1990.

Elam, Keir. "Not I: Beckett's Mouth on the Ars(e) Rhetorica." In Enoch Brater, ed., *Beckett at 80/Beckett in Context.* New York and Oxford: Oxford University Press, 1986, p. 124.

Engel, Lehman. *The Making of a Musical.* New York: Macmillan Publishing Co., 1977.

Evans, Everett. Review of *The Lorca Play. Houston Chronicle* (25 April 1992), sec. D, p. 3.

———. "The Work of 'Angels.' " Arts Notes [column], *Houston Chronicle* (16 April 1995), sec. D, p. 1, 12.

———. " 'Perestroika' Maintains Its Brilliance." *Houston Chronicle* (21 April 1995), 10, 17, 18.

Evans, G. Blakemore. *The Riverside Shakespeare*. Boston: Houghton Mifflin, 1974.

Gibson, Ian. "Juvenilia, 1917–18." *Federico Garcia Lorca: A Life*. New York: Pantheon Books, 1989.

Giffin, Glenn. " 'Carmen' Frills Cut by Brook." *Denver Post* (2 July 1995), sec. E, p. 7.

Goldstein, Melvin. Review of "The Brooklyn Conference." *The Shakespeare Newsletter*. Quoted in Glenn Loney, ed. *Staging Shakespeare: Seminars on Production Problems*. New York: Garland Publishing, 1990.

Gottfried, Martin. "The Concept Musical." *New York Times* (25 April 1972), sec. 2, p. 1–5.

Haun, Harry. "The 'Class' Act." *Playbill* 14, no. 2 (30 November 1995): 20–22.

Herles, Wolfgang. "Cosi son Tutte—Oder: Tschecow und der Feminismus." Review of *Three Tall Women*. *Der Standard* (17 June 1992): 12.

Heumann, Scott F. Review of *Willie Stark*. *Opera News* 46 (August 1981): 30.

Hodgins, Paul. Review of *Master Class*, *The Orange County Register* (19 May 1995) in Mark Taper Forum, Los Angeles, CA, p. 310.

Holland, Bernard. "A 'Carmen' in Microcosm." *New York Times* (13 March 1995), sec. C, p. 14.

"Hot Type." *Chronicles of Higher Education* (23 June 1995), sec. A, p. 11.

Jacobson, Robert J. Review of *Ashmedai*. *Opera News* 44 (June 1976): 32.

———. Review of *Silverlake*. *Opera News* 44 (June 1980): 30.

Kerr, Walter. Review of *Cabaret*. *New York Times* (21 April 1971), sec. 2, p. 1–5.

Kissel, Howard. *David Merrick: The Abominable Showman (The Unauthorized Biography)*. New York/London: Applause Books, 1993.

Klaus, Carl H., Miriam Gilbert, Bradford S. Field, Jr. *Stages of Drama*. 2nd ed. New York: St. Martin's Press, 1991.

Kolin, Philip, ed. *Conversations with Edward Albee*. Jackson and London, University of Mississippi Press, 1988.

Kramar, Konrad. "Vienna's English Theatre: Neuer Edward Albee: Hozernes Stuck Theater." Review of *Three Tall Women*. *Neuer Kronen Zeitung* (16 June 1991), 36.

Kroll, Jack. "Concerto for Diva," *Newsweek* (13 November 1995). Reprinted in *National Theatre Critics' Reviews* 56: 554.

Kushner, Tony. "Is It a Fiction That Playwrights Create Alone?" *New York Times* (21 November 1993), sec. II, p. 1, 30–31.

Lahr, John. "Dead Souls." Review of Arthur Miller's *Broken Glass*. *New Yorker* 70, no. 12 (9 May 1994): 94, 95, 96.

Leithauser, Brad. "Legend of the Fall." *Time* (10 November 1995). Reprinted in *National Theatre Critics' Reviews* 56: 561.

Loney, Glenn, ed. *Staging Shakespeare: Seminars on Production Problems*. New York and London: Garland Publishing Co., 1990.

Luere, Jeane. "An Elegy for Thwarted Vision." Review of Edward Albee's *The Lorca Story: Scenes from a Life*. *Journal of Dramatic Theory and Criticism*. University of Kansas, New York (Spring 1995): 142–147.

Luere, Jeane. Review of *Three Tall Women*. *Theatre Journal* 44 (Spring 1992): 250–52.

Luere, Jeane, and Sidney Berger, eds. *Playwright versus Director*. Westport, CT: Greenwood Press, 1994.

M., Syd. "Premier Premiere." Review of *Three Tall Women*. *Woodstock Times* 2 (6 August 1992): 7.

McNally, Terrence. "Edward Albee in Conversation." In Philip Kolin, ed. *Conversations with Edward Albee*. Jackson and London: University of Mississippi Press, 1988.

Morley, Sheridan. "London Ticket." *Playbill* (November 1995), 26.

"Now Playing on Broadway." *Playbill: The National Theatre Magazine*, 15, no. 9, 30 June 1997: 34–35.

O'Neill, Eugene. Introduction, *Selected Plays of Eugene O'Neill*. New York: Random House, 1967.

Pacheco, Patrick. "Standing Tall." *Playbill: The National Theatre Magazine* 10 (31 July 1994): 38.

Richards, David. "Edward Albee and the Road Not Taken." *New York Times* (16 June 1991), sec. 2, p. 19.

Roberts, Vera Mowry, Alice M. Robertson, and Millie S. Barranger. *Notable Women in the American Theatre*. Westport, CT: Greenwood Press, 1989.

Rodgers, Richard. *Musical Stages: An Autobiography*. New York: Random House, 1978.

Roudané, Matthew C. *Public Issues, Private Tensions: Contemporary American Drama*. New York: AMS Press, 1993.

———. *Who's Afraid of Virginia Woolf?: Necessary Fictions, Terrifying Realities*. New York: G. K. Hall, 1990.

———. Review of *The Man Who Had Three Arms*. In Harold Bloom, ed. *Modern Critical Views: Edward Albee*. New York: Chelsea House Publishers, 1987.

Samuels, Steven. "Yes Is Better Than No." *American Theatre Magazine* (September 1994), 38.

Savran, David. Quoted in "Hot Type." *Chronicles of Higher Education* (23 June 1995), sec. A, p. 11.

Schneider, Alan. *Entrances*. New York: Viking Penguin Inc., 1986.

Shine, James G. "Albee Play Meets Tall Expectations." *Kingston Freeman News* (15 August 1992), sec. 2, p. 7.

Sievers, David. Excerpt from "Realizations of the Scope of the Theatrical Productions." In *Directions for the Theatre*, 1974, pp. 11–12.

Sievers, W. David, Harry E. Stiver, Jr., and Stanley Kahan. *Directing for the Theatre*. 3rd ed. Dubuque, Iowa: William C. Brown Publishers, 1974.

Simon, John. "The Good Maria." *New York* 28, no. 46 (20 November 1995): 88–89.

Stanislavsky, Constantin. *My Life in Art*. J. J. Robbins, trans. New York: Theatre Arts Books, 1948.

Sucher, C. Bernd. "All the Rest Is Chatter." *American Theatre* 12, no. 4 (April 1995): 18.

Swanston, Hamish F. "More Verdi Than Ever." *Opera News* 58, no. 14 (2 April 1994): 8–10.

Thrall, William, Addison Hibbard, and C. Hugh Holman. *A Handbook to Literature*. New York: Odyssey Press, 1960.

Tierney, Margaret. "Jumping at Lady Hamilton: Zoe Caldwell Talks to Margaret Tierney." *Plays and Players* (October 1970), 20.

Weeks, Janet. "Kushner's 'Angels' Called a Watershed in American Theatre." *Los Angeles Daily News* (10 September 1995), sec. D, p. 6–7.

Williams, Tennessee. "Afterword" to *Camino Real*. Norfolk, Conn.: New Direction Books, 1953. (Now published in *Where I Live*, copyright 1953 by Tennessee Williams.)

Zamponi, Linda. "Von Der Tragodie des Altwerdens." Review of *Three Tall Women*. *Die Presse* (19 June 1991): 37.

Index

ISBN 0-313-30050-X

EAN

9 780313 300509

HARDCOVER BAR CODE

About the Editors

JEANE LUERE is Professor Emeritus of Theatre at the University of Northern Colorado. She has published extensively in the fields of English literature and the humanities. Her previous books include *Playwright vs. Director* (Greenwood, 1994). Her articles have appeared in journals such as *Studies in American Drama: 1945–Present, South Atlantic Review*, and *Theatre Journal*.

SIDNEY BERGER is John and Rebecca Moores Professor and Director, School of Theatre, University of Houston. He is also the founder and Producing Director of the Houston Shakespeare Festival and the Children's Theatre Festival. Recently inducted into the College of Fellows of the American Theatre at the Kennedy Center, Dr. Berger has extensive professional directing experience, including productions at the Alley Theatre, where he served as an associate artist, at Theatre Under the Stars, and at Stages Repertory Theatre. He was also awarded the Mayor's Arts Award for Outstanding Contribution by a Performing Artist.